PLATTER

The Songlines of **Chris Mosdell**

HEAD

SPLATTERHEAD

The Songlines of **Chris Mosdell**

E P
E
Emerson's Eye Press

EP
Emerson's Eye Press
a BentLight Media Imprint

Boy Abyss wrote these Gnarl Yarns for the Immutable 'A' and the Young
Yelpers, with a little arcane-assisted jolt therapy from the Iconoclastic
Hatchettes, the Neophytes of Null, euphoric tinctures, jugs of synapse
julep, and the infinite energy orgies in the Shooting Sap Asylum.

In this edition, extracts from *The Yelp House Kantos* have been given
titles and *Invisible Fire for the Innocent* and acts from the libretto
LAA... have been purposefully edited.

Visual Engineering: Mercury Design Group; www.MercuryDG.com
Front cover photos: Julie Lees/Yasushi Akiba
Back cover photo: Yuji O/Iden Graphics

Library of Congress Cataloging-in-Publication Data

ISBN 1-893722-02-3

TABLE OF CONTENTS

from CITY OF SONG: The Incendiary Arias

from THRILLS IN VOIDVILLE

from THE EROTIC ODES AND ANTHEMS

from THE YELP HOUSE KANTOS

from THE 88 INTENSITIES: A Book of Charms

from THE ROAR ROOMS

from THE THRONG SONGS: A Book of Chants

from INK MUSIC

from LIVING ON ROAR STREET WITH THE WORLD AND HIS WIFE

from LAA... The Dangerous Opera Begins

from WRITING THE RIOT ACT IN THE ILLITERATE HOUR

I have Howl Knowledge
I have Intensity Shrapnel Scars to show it
I have screaming oracles
I have a Delirium Diploma to prove it

The flaming erotic phoenix is shrieking
All its firesongs repeating
As through the aisles we charge—
The last of the Everlasting Shards

SPLATTER HEAD

from
CITY OF SONG
The Incendiary Arias

THRONG SONG

I

Blood tides, we are their names
The pulse's pound of the mute Sluice Tribes
Ol' navigators of the Great Gnarled Line
Sumptuous futures carved on our eyes

So come, street-bleatin' creatures, skin-winged easels
Oblivion weasels, anonymous ether
Come, the blur-furred in the viscous herd
Come, the devouring day of the Erosive Age
The cellular surge through the blathering world

We are the blood tides
That rise and fall
As tangled tides on a senseless shore
We are the blood tides
That spill their sides
In a gush 'n' a great cataleptic roar

In a gush 'n' a great cataleptic roar

AORTA AVENUE

For it is written:
In your gravity harness you will plunge into the skies
Your flowering blood will carpet the Roar Glade
Your walking will weave a litany mat
And tongues will be tangled into cacophony braids

I bless you with the sign of the Dyslexic Drumrun through the Gilded Skull
I bless you with the sign of the Thorn Shoes and the Fire Slippers
I bless you with the sign of the Scar Boy in the Choir of Braille Wailers
I bless you with the sign of the Harvester of Riot Berries

For it is written:
The twisted street will be straightened
The wan face will be coloured in flaring anointments
The howling head will be quieted
Parched skin will be smothered in quenching scents

See, it is I who rides blindsaddled with the scribes
I am jacked up on void noise, eel fevers, stupor juice, drunken rumbas,
    and birth glows

For it is written:
The winged stones will come flying in
The disturbed will be usurped by a rapturous calm
Those who wait will be bright human bait
Coated in magma musk and slaughter balm

I bless you with the sign of the Toothed Vision and the Singing Spines
I bless you with the sign of the Albino Ideas in the Coma Clubs
I bless you with the sign of the Machinery of Soothing, the Medicine
    of the Nil Pills
I bless you with the sign of the Great Globular Breasts of Succor

For it is written:
The buckled and bruised will be incarnated spangled and sequined

4

There will be the birth of the Alluring Icon of Eternity
The clamp suits will be loosened and necks will be freed
There will be smug-rugs to lie on and energy entrails to read

Jewels will stud the cheekbones, swoon-stones the lips
The drinkers of darkness will swell with light
While those who recite the Ruckus Catechism will be immune
To the beautiful jackal bullets and the Kingpins of Spite
And I will pass in long strides over Aorta Avenue
Combing little frenzies into my crown
Sharing where the static songlets live
And the quivering atomic constellations shine down

I bless you with the sign of the Golden Rampage Fountain Spilling the Tribes of Blather
I bless you with the sign of Ungirdled Delirium, Mouth Ziggurats, Scream Realms
I bless you with the sign of the Recipes for the Steaming Hormone Pie
I bless you with the sign of the Blizzard Tunnels through the Visceral Homeland
I bless you with the sign of Mother Volatility with her Passions Geysers Howling
I bless you with the sign of the Three Hundred Finned Elation Jacket
    worn by Kid Cataclysm

I am jacked up on void noise, eel fevers, stupor juice, drunken rumbas,
    and birth glows
I bless you with these signs—you who are skin-stained and exposed
I am jacked up on void noise, eel fevers, stupor juice, drunken rumbas,
    and birth glows
I bless you with these signs—fecund friends, go, grow

LET ME RIDE THROUGH THE WRECK AGE IN A SPASM JUDDERNAUT

Let me sleep in your deep and loving furnace
Let me be pierced by the Bullets of Blare
Let me ride through the Wreck Age in a spasm juddernaut
Let the lullabies of light spit out through the air

Let me be dressed in sparkling supernova wear
Let the wilderness decibels ring from my hips
Let me be topped in Epileptic Urgency Fountains
Let the juice of frenzy fruit stain my lips

I have been crowned
The Soft and Succulent Species
The Great Glimmer of the Energy Isle
Beautiful and breathing
Ms. Darling Devastation all aflicker
With swooping eyelids, maelstrom-milk fed
Sweet skin drumbaby of inertia worship
Slither fun and blood juggling in an exploding head

Let the splinters of the stampediatricks anoint my eyes
Let the fiery thrill-tonics work their ways
Let me spoon down eclipse-splits and disappear with a sigh
Let me go out in a devastating flowering blaze

I have been crowned
The Soft and Succulent Species
The Great Glimmer of the Energy Isle
Beautiful and breathing
Ms. Darling Devastation all aflicker
With swooping eyelids, maelstrom-milk fed
Sweet skin drumbaby of inertia worship
Slither fun and blood juggling in an exploding head

OUTSIDE THE NAKED NONSENSE IS CRASHING

Come among my sacred scalps, Great Hunter
Leave your blunt diseases beyond the door
It's the strength of my earthly scent that you're aching for
As you drag yourself in from the River of Roars

Start with a cup of the serenity stuff
Swig it down in one swift slug
Soothing soma for your dilapidation
Jagged-joy snuff that will swim through your blood
The Absolute Elation Drug

Outside the naked nonsense is crashing
There's a scattering, a shattering, an uprooting in the road
Outside the naked nonsense is crashing
But there is calm in this sanctuary I own

O Great Hunter, let me scalp you now
By laying a kiss upon your brow
We'll do the Rot Trot around the room
Baby Blizzard, it's just me and you
It might look ruined and pretty crude
But it'll cure the darkness of your life-sized bruise

Outside the naked nonsense is crashing
There's a scattering, a shattering, an uprooting in the road
Outside the naked nonsense is crashing
But there is calm in this sanctuary I own

FIRE WIGS IN THE HOUSE OF LIFE

Baby Jitter's in erotic neon freckles, unhitched eyeballs 'n' Acute
    Beauty Mortal Weapons
Spouting magic-slink formulae in the Bliss Pit's Punch Out
Slipping elliptical alligator argon in the ears, U-turn flesh bullets for the
    Salivator Louts

They're doing the Hag Waltz under the Sphincter Sun (squeal weasels of fun)
Miss Peristalsis, stained in rotten aeon lotion, does the Veins and Arteries Tease
The Sacred Spleens singing their hit: "Noxious Noctune in C"

In the House of Life they're wearing fire wigs tonight
The Siren Fathers, kings in Ovary Antlers, with encephalitic blight
Snapping nipples in the Isle of Stunned Atoms
The Loin Bosses strutting their 12-gauge squirm guns, ho-hum!

O fire wigs in the House of Life... cockscombs alight

Under the roof the Eterniity Sickness rages
The Decoy Boys pretending to be Chinese sages
Melt Downers and Comas roam around town
Making overloaded ocelot and icky iguana sounds

In the House of Life they're wearing fire wigs tonight
Funky orgasmic dialects at their whip-pitched height
Spunky Young Utopians dance the Decapitation
Spooked on nebulae dust and eliolation

O fire wigs in the House of Life... cockscombs alight

THE SUGAR SHARK

O the sugar shark, the sugar shark
Has a softness in his slaughter
See how he swims in silence
Around your lovely daughters
In and out the great street's reef
With a glint in his teeth
Sniffing out the scents in the warm night's waters

Come, long-legged flesh fish
Through the wild weeds of this lagoon
Come and see the sugar shark
In his suit of oyster blue
Enter in your shoals, in your shiny gills of gold
Let all your little scales of light
Come unhooked tonight

Let all your little scales of light
Come unhooked tonight

UH!
THE BLARE RAID OF THE ATOMIC PLEASURE SQUADRON

I

Awake in the baffled nuptial hour, fire-fingers sprouting on the skin as I sing:

Strike me with the Iconoclastic Hatchettes in spleen guns carousing through the
spoils of the Eruptive Order, down the Torso Run, concussion-gear, incendiary
hoopla plumage, and young yelpers' apprenticeship buttons sparkling

Strike me with a body-bladed climaxe cleaving the coma-crown, the harem shamen
spawning it up in the bliss-bath with euphoria tinctures, inferno infections,
and jugs of synapse julep

Strike me in the Big Barbarous, where the pollinators are thick and there is
unsheathed hunger spearing and I, ol' warrior wordsmith of the Gnarl Yarns,
have found another ear to swoop into, to ring the vaults with bellow fever
arsenal and endangered rhyme-spasm

Strike me with trigger-happy breasts pointing off into the ninty-nine cores of
oblivion

Strike me with the smitherinas in the lunge-halls, the shriek pastures teeming with
unleashed maniac species making beelines for the radiation parlors where
there are dark and wispy thinking things of counterfeit beauty lolling

Strike me with the Neophytes of Null, nymph-flares on sex-stilts pouring up
Southern Frenzy Street with eyelids stained in blur-baby opiates and glaze
howlette blue

Strike me with blazing birth drugs jumping hurdles in the soul

Strike me as the Crescendo Chiefs, flexing aura-hulks on erotic deep-ease unguents,
sockets blurting ghetto-gasps in the Great Disembowelment Bazaar, drive roar
wagons through the hour's hymen with Eternity Boy dead in the corner

Strike me with the 500th Law of Deplorability as I sit at the Raw Ranch with the
lithe blab-breeds spiking their mouths with fester-juice distilled from the wild
flophouse berry

Strike me in the Arena of the Inane Aromatics, succulent landscapes of denudity and
flowery deluges of milky urgency, shambled exquisitries, flak-scars in the
phantasmagoric funnels, the rage coach loaded with the SynchroNation,
womb-lingo, stretch-flesh, and ebbheads flickering in their celestiality with
maximum slum damage and scalped singing jangling in the wind

Strike me in the throat with the mating yodel, the whistle of the rutting psycho-stag and the rumble of all the Eternal Yearnings, the Ultimate Uns, pierced pubescence, zero-smokers, immaculata artillery of the Fallopians standing in starved contortions on the rooftops, absolute vapor-apers in nuclear ointment on the shag heaps

Strike me with full-throttle eclipses written over the skin with the wanton thrill-quill, the Albino Gland Patrol hit-and-stunning, proboskissing, jacking on and off sterile-style in the fire-riding schools and the swoon campuses

Strike me with acrobatic intoxicants making spine-gysers plume through the clotted air over Skull Island

Strike me with omni-amnesia darts, predatory Labyrinthines, faith poultices and the Incomprehensible Amulet hung around the rank emaciated Aeon Abductress

Strike me with neutronic Identikids exchanging Jets-of-Lag, hover-dope, anti-erasures, the League of the New Volcanics campaigning for a Scorched Birth Policy of the Erotic Delta down the telepaths in barb bells and ceremonial stings

Strike me in the Urge Lair as I sip crackling cortex cocktails and pop gusto-pills

Strike me at my barren Exposure Point when the Flying Jolt Boys on Enlightenment Rampages are whooping in the furnace

Strike me with the harmonics of the Obliteration Ringers whose braided dialogues weave a strangulation of stories in the name of the Great Mutated Mother

Strike me with stiff-suits tooting wipe-out cheroots in the Towers of Obedience and racing in rituals through the Illicit Isle of Utterance, yanking the brain-reins with spice-warp and smut-snuff

Strike me with emblematic cock-kings cawing their angel edicts over the kingdom (singing *The Ruckus Lymph Lullaby*) as the manlimbs jerk with shine-reflexes on lewdfoods steaming on the plate

Strike me with crash-pallors, ravage-rouge, and odyssey-orbs staking out the fornication forerunners who flash their famous invisible phylacteries in the Rude Nook and other basement trick joints

Strike me with spunk-stabs to sear the Seer and allow the wail-odes to flourish in the Shooting Sap Asylum

Strike me with those who are planted in messianic meditation on the curb, Annihilation of the Ages pumping through the sluice gates to feed the Ghost Choir of Fresh Enchantments with the new spirit of the Lust Generation

Strike me on a leash in my tugging to horizones and futurities twinkling in their abyss-attire and flirt-nipples, beckoning, the scepter raised to whore-roar sun in a fecundity skirt to the arse

Strike me with meteoritic gut weaponry, the quandaries of the Sloth States, the squeal-trimmed Damnzealots, screwballers, cornucopian kiosks, and the Great Churn Pant-o-mime rancid with cosmic tan, bare shin-din, and apoplectic bunnypies

Strike me with the readings: *Spawn Ethics, The Novocane Whippings, Pyroman, The Cult Organism, Rumble Jugglers,* and *The Illustrated Thrust Manual*

Strike me with the tingling hybrid knowledge fed to the Splatbrats with their boom-immunity, roaming through the balmy fumes spiked on overloads of decibella, sugary writhe dollops and haywire aphrodisiacs

Strike me with randy-floss hairdos, the Gash Fashions of the Oh Zone, murder mascara, gleaming sonic braces, and a plague of smug-addictions

Strike me with the flaming tome of the Almighty Amok Literature spouting forth, the Little Fertilizers in their exposures, the egocenters, the Absentias in spark-arc halos, slugging pow-venom on Underbelly Street, trance parasites exploding in their hoax hats at angles of utter delirium

Strike me with the Children of Dilapidated Ubiquity, chromatic tops, ultimate earth-edge junkies with rotten symmetry, centipediastry, the Neuter Looters doing the Stagnant, the Garb Age, mummified in noise wax

Strike me with giant idiotgrams blazing, giddy distempers, eyes popped with magic friction, branded bodies of swampy sacredness riddled through, the stinging signs pelting, spitting, piercing me with narcotic rattle, the cataclysmic shakes

Strike me in the Great Foetal River with inertia-shades steamed up, alight amongst the Ember Members, ashen on exhaustion fixes with the homeward infinity crawlboys

Strike me on my rickety Skeletonic Statue weathered by a million warrior varmints, riot rain, the Pretty Erosives flaying their whip-wigs and immortalists illuminating the everlasting blankness with joy-juice included

Strike me as I ride the Disrupter, prince of speed aeons with my fecund friend wrapped around my neck screaming the antisocial argot of millennia

Strike me as the Powman of the Phallic Furrow, Embalmer of the Om-Om Drum, feasting on buxsoma, narcoticking in fetish paint around the Erogenous Allotment of the neighborhood

Strike me with the Siren of Absolute Earthly Epileptica atop the Blunder Bus reeling in transient marketplaces of mutation, the Twang Dynasty in the last throes of paralysis selling twitch-wear and flame-tufts for the Wired Brigade

Strike me with the grand opening of the Cryptic Canteen, serving fleshpot holes, virgin killerwatts, cyburgers, sticky art-tarts for the famine that rages outside among the knots, and hypersonia and intensity aromas ricocheting up and down the universe, permeating the very fabric of the civil orbits

Strike me in the Abyss Mall encrusted with cyclo-soma trophies, techquiller shots to sooth the Devilry Daddies, jagged gene punks of the Bombardment Beltway, Excess-in-Amber Ramblers, syrupy catalytic anointments exploding on the brow

Strike me in this Haunted Hive with the vigor-triggers, sperm-herders, Glutters, vampiric hoodwinkers in the dark veindrain, Larval Derelictables in dreamland, metamorphosing into the spooky New Emptiness

Strike me with the Bliss Trysters, the frisky porn-bucks in stimulation stampedes, exploring their neuro-nets in the scrums, their deep covens, mucous mouths all baited, waiting for a bite of ecstasy icing, to be shot, blamming, expectant to ceiling wastelands in the cells

Strike me in Blankjack Joints, once rank with cellar scent, rapid static, skin-tight striders with prehensile numb-tongues, now virus k.o.s, rot rhythmics and the ruined chimes clanking in the exterminating air

Strike me with the Golden Seizures smoking octave jets, blotto on nova yolks, alien funk circuits with wave after wave of heat jerky surging into the Big Dismal

Strike me in the Intimate Assassination Galaxy where incandescent catatonic symptoms shudder through the Pure Pestilence Primthings and the Skin-Alives hang out on the kooky kemical clothesline and experience exotic implosions of absolute euphony

Strike me with Hyp Hallucinogenies plummeting down shock-holes in high-wheeled shoes, wounded metabolicks, manikinships, excellent junk allahs crawling through the dark adultery

Strike me in the Throngdom while awaiting new gadgetry to spur the eyes, electronic excrement bursting out and enormous encephalitic alterations stripped to their undressed identities

Strike me with Nowboys in the myth-mixer, autopsy turby swamps to sink into, where the swollen and the erect Solar Plexus Rangers are accosting the legendary oozing muffs in the short-shaved outskirts

Strike me in the Throb Station with the Action Orkids in flexible orgasm girdles, rot-nosed lush-lynxes sniffing double-barrelled Absence, the Big Bastard Circus ablaze with the Miasmics on bioillogic prescriptions, hermaphroditic germ-juice, mega-mating vibrations, and cooing rites

Strike me with electro-cute dumbslingers and sweet Dyslexables spangled in damaged silence, immaculate thought conspiracies, and weave hells

Strike me with interplanetary bitch pistols, the Split Peons, Hemorragers, mashed spur-songs leaking from the Tangled Temple reflected in the plaguepool

Strike me with brow-breaking howl-wreaths practicing their tribal permutations, energy-gelders helmeted and decorated in ultra-shambles, din-striped uniforms in the Alternative Oven

Strike me with the Contagious Copulation Orchestra thrashing, conception hotels, epidemic ambushes of the serrated senses, looters of immortality acid sharing spoils in the Phosphorescent Center

Strike me with gimmick diseases: frockpox, grotto tongue, tribe writhe, nasty plasma romp fever, and all the allergies of the eternal sub-spine sewage

Strike me with the Magnificent Mystic Masseurs, over-ripe cruisers in groin vessels, tattooed teeth, nausears filled with wail-hail, pummeling the legendary Captain Corpse of the Slang Gang, light fathoms and shadowy filth sharks in season

Strike me with the ol' Sugar Shrapnels, the slippery mercury maids incubating in the dark groan-toned Thought Nurseries where the Ecstasy Dictator, reeking of

rogue metabolism, riot tonic, and asylum vaccine, is the fossil adolescent, the
   Young Inorganic of Infinity
Strike me with the Extinct Libido-do Express, adrenalean and alcohollow in whoa-
   clothes, vice appendix bursting forth through the last amputated hour
Strike me within the shitty limits, ProtoplasMick, the Hexed Symbol in the Zombee
   Hive, the Immense Fertilizers, rude gut pupas, cherry bosoms, multileveled
   blackouts from vulva spurt signals at the entrance to the Brutal Neuter
Strike me with industrial miscarriages, embryonic yells in the Screw Sanctum,
   bitch-mist, swimming drool, wholesome chain-stroking at the flesh turnstile,
   the SpeciMen on gangsteroids petting beautiful plundertails
Strike me with the Vacancy Booties, speak-teasies slugging grog-spawn, extension
   antennae blinking for their Automates, pulse phones, Ol' Overdose
   Phantommy in the halo-house, down the electroads, cooking mainline con-
   menus, cogno-repellent smeared nulldozers, ataxia rushes, and lurid schizo-
   scars from all angles
Strike me with the entire population in rape tiaras and runt upholstery, Nicoteeny
   Tots, writhe-wise and swoon-tuned on the pick up for bleached
   idiocy-amputees in the racket fumes
Strike me with young hunger machines, subliminal strippers in drum-pulp cages,
   ecto-energy jackets spitting hermetic formulae, the Cockoons on steaming
   VaniTea, aortic errands, and marrow magma ('n' pa 2)
Strike me with iridescent satellite saucies adorned with vibrating breastpoints,
   apparatus exposure cruising at fury altitudes, slobber lagoon and Ms.
   Disintergrateful up the spinal staircase in flesh-hatching instruments
Strike me with the Rearranged Matriarchs in the Trauma Stadium, robe grafts, thigh
   weddings, the Atomic Pleasure Squadron pickled and shredded with desolate
   odors, slime loudspeakers, aroused strata, exquisite haunted focus in the
   beginning long ago...

Uh!

II

Uh! Miraculous Throat-Turbines! Uh! Whoremoans! Uh! The Astronomical
Swaddling Show Entertaining Rapt Guilloteens! Uh! Vapor Males Imploding
Igneous Cargoes into Varicose Fast-Lanes! Uh! Mechanical Mastiffs Unleashed on
the Rabies Babies! Uh! Squirmers in Flesh Enhancers! Uh! Enormous Ikonic Ruckus
Coiffures! Uh! Inertia Serum Swigging at Birth Rites in the Karma Harem! Uh!
Scrubdom! Uh! Dear Little Distortion Kits Packed with Hypothalamic Pluckers,
Castrating Clippers! Uh! Doing the Riptease At The Great Gurgling Gut Hut! Uh!
The Anointments of the Exotique Acids! Uh! The Rotating Skullcaps of the Youth
Grenades! Uh! Queen Phoenix and the Sex-Rays! Uh! The Anonymous Mental
Ejaculators in Vulture Shock! Uh! Slurmaids in Sting-Stick Holsters! Uh! Plagues of
Maulpox! Uh! New Bile Twitch Lingo! Uh! Aphrodisiattacks Along Decay Way!
Uh! Comet Wheelchairs Through the Sacred Scrimmage! Uh! High Stung Ultra-

Clutters Around the Fact Racks! Uh! Pulse Candy! Uh! Ms. Undulation in Vibrating Bodysocklet! Uh! Erotic Earth Quaker, the Atrocious Lotus! Uh! Up the Spine Gutters into the Wandering Womb Clubhouse! Uh! Blasting Vigor Mortis in the Bruise Booths! Uh! The Progeny Rush! Uh! Idiocy Aisle, the Wondrous Spew Center! Uh! Smashed Whirlwindows! Uh! Pearl-Skinned Decoys with Double-Barrelled Anatomy Signaling Derangement! Uh! Altered Ovals, Dappled Ectoplasm Citi-Zens! Uh! Salivation Rituals in the Big Wide Leprosea! Uh! Slime Time! Uh! Genetic Saturation Street! Uh! Paroxysm Pie Splattered over the Walls of Libido Lounge! Uh! Skull Impersonators in Serpent Suits! Uh! The Neutered Varmint Yelping for Miss Chief! Uh! Absolute Paralysis from the Dome Down from Celibacy Gadget Worship! Uh! Practicing Confragationalists! Uh! Oblivion Keepers in the Cardinal Din! Uh! Hybrid Scent Machettes Sweetened on Siren Sieges, Kool Go-Vacant Condiments! Uh! Displaced Taut-Assed Impervious Drool Pigeons Gobbling Up Longevity Capsules! Uh! Commando Bitch Blossoms Seizing Jolt-Waggons and Whisking Away to Embryo Stores! Uh! Deliveries of Slobber! Uh! Neo-Astro Attire of the Obscene Object, the Hornimental Geishaaah! Uh! Gaggles of Pinup Blackout Babes Sipping Ceremonious Stud-Blood in the Insemination Arena! Uh! Celestial Assistants Stripping Off with Eye Socket Spasms! Uh! Procession of the Ghost Generation! Uh! The Disability Dance! Uh! Diagnosed with Pointless Poison Seizures! Uh! Fetishistic Hunting for Translucent Wriggling Immaculata on Sex Placebos! Uh! Jeweled Tongues In The Screw Menagerie! Uh! Twisted Fever Vessels Navigating the Extraordinary Inflammable Shambles! Uh! Scar Nodheads Smoking and Impregnating Miracle Musk! Uh! Incandescent Glands Spurting Divine Magic Milk! Uh! Ran Sid, the Rotter in Doom-Doped Fingernails! Uh! Mayhem Muzzles! Uh! The First Virginal Deformities Lead into the Place of the Afterbirth in Electrified Bridles! Uh! The Performing Aortahs! Uh! Null Dust Cloud Inhalation! Uh! Quivering Visceralia Probes Registering Every Instinctive Ablution of the Toxin Tribes! Uh! It's Reek Week for the Replicats! Uh! The Sigh Clones Are Bedded! Uh! Slugs of Organ Disembodiment Wine Gurgling Through the Wreck Meats! Uh! The Sunken Cerebrals Singing the Star Spangled Bladder from the Depths of Their Circuitry! Uh! Grotto Eyepots Blinking, Ah, Decapitation Diseases! Uh! Strapping on Pelvic Spurs and Welded Corporeal Calipers! Uh! Consummation Prongs at the Ready in the Atrophied Dawn Sutra! Uh! The Entwined Kind Wrapped in Salivator Scarves! Uh! Nightcaps of Pounded Gene Beans, Sap-Zap, Truth Poppers to Hit the Spot! Uh! The Vim Thing, the Promised Man, Lolling in a Deactivation Cradle, a Real Death Eternity Buddy Through God Goggles! Uh! A New Gunflower of a Nation Growing Through the Beastly Effluvia, Underage Bedthugs, Abortive Uterines, Palpitators Trafficking Psychic Flesh Fungi, Debacle Therapy, Sterilizing Clang-Concoctions and Rising Above on His Periscopic Neck, His Sharpened Specter, His Ineffable Auguries, the Golden Gibberist! Uh!

I'M A CREATURE OF EXOTIC INTENSITY

In my squawk shirt
I wake the earth
I'm a creature
Of exotic intensity
The siren of ol' Snarl Street
And O the rustling randomness
Of each green and growing need

To shine in a crown of howls
Through the savageries of town
The lynxboys on their chains
Lust for my living glade

In my squawk shirt
I wake the earth
I'm a creature
Of exotic intensity
As I swoop out of my skies
And on raw and brutal passions feed
Among the jade made trees

IN THIS RIVER I'LL BE HIS ROCK

The line is straight
The wool is dyed
The Word, a star of light
In these dark-drumming times

To be fed by this light is a glorious thing
Let the seemless sky cleave and sing

Deliver us from the pout-house dildolls
In their skin-bells ripe and ringing
From the squeal hips and the lulu tongues
The painted frillies with their nipple guns
And the drool dance, the crude shoes
The spasm madames, the lewd brood
And the sugar tarts who bake their art
On Slop Street through the dark
From the howlheads in their thickets
The wallow worms of the wicked
The cravers and lusting razors
Faith thieves, sin sailors
The swoon spoons and the brazen
And every bleating leering lamb
Across this blistered land

Until these fevers leave the flock
In this river I'll be His rock

In this river I'll be His rock

In this river I'll be His rock

THE WATER'S WOMB

I rise from the rice
From the water's womb
To erupt in your eyes
Old ways flaring anew

From the sterile swamp
The mad mud, the junk pools
On tiny fertility feet
Among the rootless spew

The phallic chalice is spilling seed
Pods explode, bellies burst
The first lust buds appear
Through the groaning earth

And watch as I touch
The barren fields of your hands
And revive the green fires
Once the backbone of this land

ONWARDS THROUGH
THE GREAT BLURRED WORLD

I've judders in the veinlanes
Jet spouts and jab rays
Bones that know their own way
O and wilderness weather swirls
As I go happily wandering
In my gown and spinning spurs

That carry me onwards through the Great Blurred World

I'm the eager arrow of the inner bow
As I wait here I am sown
In the blue baby seas
And tall green lands
A body quite beyond speed
In this gown with a silken sheen
That moves me where I stand

And carries me onwards through the Great Blurred World

THRONG SONG

X

The Racket Songs are in our lungs
Long live these songs—they go on and on

Blissdom comes in bits and bites
Down the arteries, up the spine

The fleshy lure, what a homely scene
We come out chasing the Cyclone Queen

Six hundred sirens in our hair
Calling through the idiot air

LONG LIVE THE OBLIVION BROTHERHOOD

Long live the Oblivion Brotherhood
In the circular sutra of the blood

The clatterboys may bark and bicker
Siren Sam may block the sun
Still, the Oblivion Brotherhood's drowning drum
Will overcome, will overcome

Drowning drum, drowning drum
Come, come, come
Till the Great Peaceful Pathway Song
Proclaims the Province of the Numb

Here I stand upon the Great Roar Shore
Asking to be swept away
Where ether isles embalm my eyes
Haloed in the haze

Long live the Oblivion Brotherhood
In the circular sutra of the blood
Come, come, O drowning drum
To overcome, to overcome

O Immense Swaddling Hum along the Racket Rivers
O Splutter Song through the Tangled Throats
O Cleaving Chorus, O Wail Hail Hymn
Come Evergreen Bombardment, in one annihilating stroke

Here I stand in full eclipse-gear
My body blinkers, my thick-skin shutter
Giving birth to Odes of the Inert
In the Writhe Aisles, the spit-wrecked gutter

O long live the Oblivion Brotherhood
In the circular sutra of the blood

THE SHINING SHEPHERD OF THE DISOWNED

All you who follow in my wake
Walk the White Way, the Pristine Path, are free
As I cleave through your Bruised Jewelry
Dancing the Dreg Leg, the Shithead Waltz
The Spew, the Gruntboy Gruel
O here I come

In my arms, all the abandoned
The forlorn, the immense emaciated storm
All your treasures are mine
Under my spearing eye
Dancing the Incinerator, the Obliterator
The Crumpled, the Crashed Out
O here I come

I run through the Glut, the Rich Retch Zone
The Shining Shepherd of the Disowned
Whistling tunes of immunity
Through the Great Slop Sea

THE TALKING TATTOO UPON MY THIGH

Already on my body are the scars of eyes
My body of future wars
My body from the pearl-peach shores
Where the senses come to die
Where the talking tattoo on my thigh
Makes throats sigh
Where the talking tattoo on my thigh
Makes boys blind

Already I dangle the bait
The hook shining in the doorway
The silent spears I say
Uneaten in this ripened state
Where the talking tattoo on my thigh
Makes throats sigh
Where the talking tattoo on my thigh
Makes boys blind

You, the Starving School Sea
You, the drool boys on agony
Yes, that's what I'll do
Carve a talking tattoo on my thigh for you
Something so rude
It'll burn off your shoes

THRONG SONG

XII

In the orgies of our energies
We wade the knotted sea
Where there's flesh in the nets
Vital Spines in the splatter-nest
Where we ride in our vixen vehicles
In our skull-guns of miracles
Where the Beautiful Discord is the law—
The ol' torn song of the Great Forlorn

So come dance the Colliding Clubfoot
Ecstasy animals under the hood
As through these aisles we charge—
The last of the Everlasting Shards

In the orgies of our energies
We are caught in the snares of the free
As we cross one curb to another
Salacious Sister, the Barking Brother
Wearing the weathers of our neglect
And the flapping coats in this homely wreck
In this Beautiful Discord that is the law—
The ol' torn song of the Great Forlorn

The flaming erotic phoenix is shrieking
All its firesongs repeating
As through the aisles we charge—
The last of the Everlasting Shards

YOU PLUNGING INFERNO-FISHERS

You plunging inferno-fishers
You swirlpool swimmers
All you stranded on the shore
You lost, adrift
You mess-dressed mariners
Who would give your kingdoms for an oar

I have boats floating
Slender and carved with erotic signs
O these eyes
I have boats leaving
Carrying the dark spices of time
O these eyes

You young debris
You wild flotsam
All you washed up by the waves
You gnarled horizons
You crumbling islands
Who are bleached by the blasts of the day

I have boats anchored
Keels to slice you through with a sigh
O these eyes
I have boats burning
Illuminating the vast dereliction of the sky
O these eyes

I FORESEE YOUR LIFE, BOY BLUR

I foresee your life, Boy Blur
In clean rays, in slash floods, in jolt worms
I'm receiving whisper-darts, voice balms
Till I'm all fiery inside with Big Eternal's burns

I foresee your life, Boy Blur
In blood races, in marrow yelps, in gut anthems
The whip frequencies flaying the air
Till the Three Fevers of Shatter Street kiss me again and again

I have Howl knowledge
I have Intensity Shrapnel Scars to show it
I have screaming oracles
I have a Delirium Diploma to prove it

I foresee your life, Boy Blur
In shafts of quiver-songs through me
The singing, a chorus in the cells
A visionary entrancing epilepsy

I have Epiphany Eruptions
I have Talking Tongues of Visceraaaah!
I have Enlightenment Antlers
Receiving skewering voices from afar

I foresee your life, Boy Blur
I'm all fiery inside with Big Eternal's burns

HER VOID HIGHNESS

I name you the Endless Eaves, the Shelter Queen
The roof over the shattered sky
Protect from thudboy-thunder and fathead fevers
And allow all to go untouched through the Leaping Gnash
And Buckled Fields of Blast

I have daubed doors and days
Bodies have awaited my indelible stain
My sign is a seal against Blister Floods and Swirling Yell Hemorrhages
That lets you survive the Deprived Rides
And soothes the frenzied eye

So when you walk down Big Rigor Road
Wear my amulet
And feel Her Void Highness
Shield and protect

I name you the Durge-proof Skin, the Persistent Thing
With words of flame-fists, bright beasts on guard
To keep away the ratty chaos-cuties and the Bash Brothers
And to allow all to go untouched through the Great Wide Rip
Where mutiny sinks the Shudder-spine Ship

So when you walk down Big Rigor Road
Wear my amulet
And feel Her Void Highness
Shield and protect

ROCKETHEAD BOOTS AT THE READY

I will float
In my phantom feathers
Through the Great Dog Delirium
With rockethead boots at the ready
To jettison from the Rooms of the Numb

Bird-bones to build a glider
Wisp-wrists in the wind
Frail fever baby in my thought wings
So ether-ankle thin

I've rockethead boots at the ready
To launch out of this mess nest
I've rockethead boots at the ready
To be off on ripped sky quests

I'm Running Ray
I'm Finned Blossom
I'm the Swift Eternal Thing
With rockethead boots at the ready
To roar off through ceilings
With rockethead boots at the ready
To race on, Dimension Stealing

I RISE TO HIGHER HALLS

I rise to higher halls
Singing deep sacredness
I am buoyed by these words
Singing deep sacredness

Farewell, Weighted Ones
With your bags and burdens
Heavy with your harvest from the Plunder Fields
This is your station—not mine
I am destined for other skylines
Among clearer turning wheels

With this recitation I rise
Singing deep sacredness
I enter realms sublime
Singing deep sacredness

Farewell, Weighted Ones
I leave you with this song

from

THRILLS IN VOIDVILLE

SPLATTERHEAD

Splatterhead
You've been drinking roar elixirs in your Doom Room again
Splatterhead
You've been spiking your cells with shiver rivers and zombie bombs again
Splatterhead
You've been dressing up in wallop scent and beauty bruises again

Splatterhead, you're a drum addict
Splatterhead, you're a screen of static
Splatterhead, you're a splintered state
Splatterhead, you're all over the place
Burst and shattered across the universe

Splatterhead
You've been experimenting with spook truths and pow pills again
Splatterhead
You've been stripping down to your rhythm scars and vista tattoos again
Splatterhead
You've been knocking back spasm shots and delirium jugs again

Splatterhead, you're a blitz stud
Eruptions under the hood
A halo of bright stilettos
You're warped, a real weirdoooo

Splatterhead, you've altered your anatomy again
O *Splatterhead*, where will you end?
Splatterhead, you're a splintered state
Splatterhead, you're all over the place
Burst and shattered across the universe

Burst and shattered across the universe

THE KING IS ON THE CLONE THRONE

I have felt the needle pierce the cell
Felt the spirit drink from the well
I have mated in the matrix
Been entwined with the serpent's helix

I felt the flood come gushing through
Long waves of whipping energy
The shutters on my eye were cleaved
And visions I have seen

And hark, the vibe vixens are howling
Rushing through me in their psychic vehicles
Chemical castles in the kingdom of the spine
Never allowing me to die
I'm Genetic Jenny in a twisted torso
With eyes of flaming hues
A touch-gun for the seventy senses
And the ecstasy engine too

And the king is on the clone throne
The solar sons are in my bones
The astrogyphs burning on my skin
Map the inward way within

I'm an angelic etherette puffing on fire
Phantom trash among the star studs
Cerebral Susie out of her mind
With warp weasels in the blood
I'm shooting up fractal fungi
The bride with piebald nuclei
Smashed out on serenity serum
Drunken on tactile tides

The king is on the clone throne
The solar sons are in my bones
The astrogyphs are burning on my skin
The king is dead, long live the king
For from his cells I sing
Sing from the kinetic cradle
Through the mosaic mouths of Babel
Beyond both good and evil
From the heights of my spiralled steeple

I have felt the needle pierce the cell
Felt the spirit drink from the well

CRASHING THE CRANIUM CAR

I am here but I am not
I am serenely still but I am shot
Through with speed splinters
I am whole but I am fractured
I am inert but I am a reactor
In the atomic plagues of my days

Clamp on the Hectic Helmet, baby
And crash the cranium car
Through the dream's dissolving wall
To the cliffs of the new warped shores

O out of time's thighs I am born
Out of the arms of an explosive dawn
Out in the molten miles
Where the ship of the body flies

Out of time's thigh I am born
As Captain Distortion on halo drugs
As the Aeon King
As the Mistress of Eternity
As the Photonic Kid with rhythm pistols blazing
As Ms. Cataclysm in stratospherical beauty booties
As a Jolt Drinker in my steaming hell suit
As oblivion-finned and howl-breasted Mother Maelstrom
As jabs of sonic juice in full flame in the veins
As Boy Abyss with his tetrahedronic trumpet
As an Orb Lord
And as every dimensional darling to grace the heavenly seas

I am single but the braided bride
I am blind but brilliantly clear-eyed
In my vista goggles of immortality
I am passive but with an ignited passion
Smooth skinned but beneath, the gene pool splashes
In a feeding frenzy of fertility

I'm crashing, I'm crashing, I'm crashing the cranium car
(*I've been drinking spectrum shots in the Blue Aura Bar*)
I'm crashing the cranium car
(*O play those gyrocryptic chords on that heliophonic guitar*)
I'm crashing the cranium car into the churning core of the stars

CRYSTAL BLURRED VIEWS OF INVISIBILITY

Let me touch your empty eyes
See how blind you've been

Now in your halo of psychic spikes
You stand on the cerebral prow
And I will place a kinetic kiss
Upon your burning brow

Now there are electron haze houses
With every molecular mod con
And coma soma on the table
To bite on and whoooosh you're gone

And the elevators of eternity
Are shooting through the ceiling
And the moment becomes molten
In the furnace of every feeling

Where the crystal-blurred views of invisibility
Die in the fires of immortality

Let me touch your sealed mind
See how blank you've been

Now your fifth eye is focusing
On the glinting fish in the plasmic pool
That swim through the reefs of the skin
In and out of you

Now your body buds and blooms
All your sense-screens are switched on and blaring
The drum juices jump up the spine
And the inferno scent you're wearing is brilliantly flaming

And the elevators of eternity
Are shooting through the ceiling
And the moment become molten
In the furnace of every feeling

Where the crystal blurred views of invisibility
Die in the fires of immortality

THE DAYS OF THE HERMAPHRONIGHTS

I'm entwined as different kinds
In the hyrbrid house inside
Beneath this scented flesh
Are ionic storms that never rest
I am the sexual schism
Of one beautiful blazing organism

I am everything that collides
The visionary and the blind
A desire unto myself
The yearning and the yelp
A blood twisted and braided
Ah, what marvels I am made of

And there's a dawning in the twilight
Where the darkness is pure and white
And I stand, a solitary twin
In the days of the hermaphronights

At the door of the Great Crave Club
Where I'm wonderfully inert
Every sense is fulfilled
From aeons before birth
And in my sea of cells
Chant all the spectrum songs
I'm a crystal that catches light
Unique among the throng

I've got tongue stings and body barbs
I've got energy hornets in the spine
I've got pulse and polarity pills
To walk a straight warped line

I'm a creation completely free
From the eruptive emotional mysteries
Perched on my pulsing throne
Balanced between the poles
I am divinely numb
In the hum of equilibrium

I am everything that collides
The visionary and the blind

THE HOLY EXPLOSIVE LINGO

I speak the holy explosive lingo of the beauty diseases
As the eternity implants along my spine shine
And I come to you laced in hormone guns
My static skirt torn open to reveal
The fiery atomic tattoos on my thighs
And the vast ecstasies of awaiting lives

SAVAGE ME WITH ULTRASONIC SENSUALITY

Pass silently through my skin
And into my own orbit spin
Where rivers of raw atoms rage
And electron clouds cascade

And let the taste of eternity
Explode upon my tongue
And let the Anthems of Intensity
Through every cell be sung

Tie me down to the wheel of heaven
Peel off my outer sheaves
Lie me down in your energy fields
Fused in perfect symmetry

O abduct me, Vortexan Voidboy
Touch me with your tactile glare
Run ecstasy frequencies through my hair
Savage me with ultrasonic sensuality
And let this carbon creature share
The swoon gun's speedy bullet
In the sumptuous Ionic Lair

O abduct me, Vortexan Voidboy
Savage me with ultrasonic sensuality
Savage me with ultrasonic sensuality

The molecularity of moans
Under the geometries of the Pleasure Dome
O flow the sacred formulae
Along the axis of a sigh

And emitting a chromatic glow
In engulfing auras of absolutes caught
Your fingers of flickering light
Beyond the horizons of human thought

THRILLS IN VOIDVILLE

Where are you going, Little Ray
With all the entrails of the day?

There are celestial cities in the burnt jade rain
Where light is twisted into a fiery braid
Where life is growing from the clay

O where are you going, Little Ray
Holding up your howling galactic flame?

There are ice blue orbits of geometry
Where the Ganglion Gangs practice symmetry
Jibing in synapse-tongues of blind velocity

O where are you going, Little Ray
With all the fragments of the day?

Over yonder horizon's hill
To search for thrills in Voidville

To search for thrills in Voidville

IN THE FURY FIELDS OF AN ATOMIC EDEN
(TRANSMISSIONS FROM THE PSYCHIC CELLAR)

Hey, you there in your psychic cellar
Strapped in your machinery
Projecting your swirling dreams
Onto the vast and starry ceiling

Meet me in the Maelstrom Slum
Meet me in the Cataclysm Club
Meet me in the Ecstatosphere
Meet me in the Zoom Room
Meet me in the Skull Stream

And bring along your drum
To bang in the vacuum

Hey, you there on Shatter Street
In your home-made inferno head-dress
Sending out codes and messages
Into the spaces, stark and endless

Meet me in the Coma Court
Meet me on Aorta Avenue
Meet me in the Burst of the Universe
Meet me on the Great Warped Way
Meet me in the Big Blank, baby

And bring along your drum
To bang in the vacuum

And in the fury fields of an Atomic Eden
Beyond the spinning reaches
Oh, earthly creature
This is where I'll meet you

Meet me in the Ether Theater
Meet me in Blam Land
Meet me in the Exploding Orbits
Meet me in the Swirl World's Wildernest
Meet me in the eclipse of every bit, babe

And bring along your drum
To bang in the vacuum

POSSESSED WITH PRISM RHYTHM

Let light pass into me
Deflect this fire through each degree
Rush through these veins
With a perfect aim

And divide me into the fields of infinity

Let light pass into me
Explode me within, splinter my skin
Shoot up my spine
Shine through my eyes

And let me seed the shores of eternity

I've energy punches in mutant motion
Shock waves across the lunar oceans
I'm the Songstress of Disorder
The lover of the stellar daughters
The universe is blinking with beauty
I'm sexual and holy neuter
A gorgeous hybrid for the voidboys
Who talk with telepathic tentacles and cataclysmic roars

I'm possessed with prism rhythm
That I howl out in helium blizzards
Dancing with the sonic lizards
Through the scaly rivers

And in the craters there are larva tongues
Wagging while the moon drums black out the sun
And the linear lovelies are swaying
The mandible dogs are baying
I've a hexagon hairdo in magnetic magenta
Magma at the center
I am the Queen of Smithereens
All shattered and plumed in steam

So take your sun gun to my head
Your light knife to my hands
Burn through my body
Scatter me through spiralled lands

I am the perfect prism
In my coat of many rhythms

SAILING THE
SEVEN TRANSPARENSEAS

I am an atom dressed in light
In my own orbit of ecstacy
I am a stone in my private silence
At the genesis of destiny

I am the howl of the burning beast
The hand of the human host
Watch as my skin now melts away
And I walk in the bones of ghosts

I am shrapnel of the soul
I am young and immensely old
I am the fetus and the grave
Interlaced through each and every age

Sailing the seven transparenseas
Diving deep down though the densities
See how I dissolve and reappear
In a higher octave to the ear

I am conscious of creation
In the singing ship of each cell
I will merge and intertwine
Into the shape of a golden bell

That rings out the Codes of the Carbon Kid
Who walks across Voidville's rickety bridge
Posing in a rare reptilian grace
One of the tribes of a solar race
Singing: "I am a ray of renegade light
A refugee of mother night
The sound of heaven's horses
Stampeding onwards through starry quarters."

Sailing the seven transparenseas
Diving deep down through the densities
See how I dissolve and reappear
A higher octave to the ear

I am conscious of creation
In the singing ship of each cell
See how I dissolve and reappear
In a higher octave to the ear

SPLATTERHEAD

from

THE EROTIC ODES AND ANTHEMS
The Love Songs of Boy Abyss

The furnace door was open
I threw myself in
Here, haloed in flame, these are the songs I sing

IN THE OBLIVION BAR, THE CATACLYSM CLUB, AND DEEP DELIRIUM DEN

In the Oblivion Bar
I found you standing there
With all your broken branches blooming with scented scars
And my instincts, leaping on their lead
Rose up and bit your thigh
And you cried out in ecstasy

And in the Cataclysm Club
I found you waiting there
Stripping down to your storms at the hormone hub
And my eyes, cutting through your immaculate chaos
Plunged right in
Until both of us were utterly lost

And in the Deep Delirium Den
I found you lying there
Dreaming of a day when the Reign of Dumb Drumming would end
And my senses, singing their anthems
Woke you wickedly
To purge all your wanton phantoms

And we sealed our scars in the Oblivion Bar
We made love in the Cataclysm Club
And did it again and again in the depths of the Deep Delirium Den
Again and again

And we rolled over the edge
As the mouth of the chasm took us in
And we merged and we moaned
Crowned on the throne of the Turmoil Twins

And we sealed our scars in the Oblivion Bar
We made love in the Cataclysm Club
And did it again and again in the depths of the Deep Delirium Den
Again and again and again

PLAY THAT OL' SINPHONY, BABY

Play that ol' sinphony, baby
Do that vulgar polka
In my private parlor
Do the Wallow
The Studded Collar
A flashy beacon to follow
Around the room
To that ol' delinquent tune

Crank up that ol' sinphony, baby
Make it loud and overbearing
Duly rude and daring
Do the Wallow
Through the squalor
Of this room
To that ol' delinquent tune

Play that ol' sinphony, baby
While I go crazy

ODE TO AN ADDICT

I have dipped my eyelashes in swoon-drugs
Lick them as I sleep
Let me awake to your addiction

SILENCE IN THE COURT OF YOUR BEAUTY

I have been sentenced to silence by the court of your beauty
I have sat with my strategies of crudity
I have carved life-sized effigies of your nudity
I have given breath to your babies in the back seat of your vixen vehicle
I have come flaming into existence
I have covered my body with apocalyptical oils
I have grown, your fecund follower, from the soil
I have sunk into the depths of darkness and leered up longingly at your light
I have scourged myself senseless at your sight
I have thrown myself, an immolated martyr, from the arch of your legs
I have chanted the catechisms of your flesh
I have been murdered by your lascivious eunuch bodyguards
I have pickled my heart in a jar
I have burnt off your fireproof dress
I have poured myself into the moulds of where you have laid
I have climbed up your fiery braid
I have shot up swoon drugs and let my veins explode
I have written the Throb Songs, the Agony Anthems, and the Erotique Odes
I have been ignored as I mimed my suicides in the Arena of Doomed Desire
I have sunk into your sultry mire
I have gilded my skin into a sacred mirror and spread-eagled myself out
    beneath your feet
I have disguised myself as your sheets
I have flown into frenzies across the engulfing chasm of your arms
I have found no immunity from your plagues of passion
    through branding my body with pornographic charms
I have lived the lives of mystical beasts, blundering, bellowing, scaly with sex
I have sealed my ears and eyes with wax and still I'm utterly wrecked
I have married the peach-hipped Goddess of Immaculata to seed
    envy in your blood
I have floated myself on an aphrodisiacal flood
I have worn my seduction spurs to break in your pearl-skinned mare
I have roamed the Den of Twisted Temptations blinded by your name
I have stood, the serpent soldier, at your side
I have felt divine flushes rush down my spine

I have been the Rude Ruckus Stud and you the Flesh-finned Slut
I have entwined barbed lust around my guts
I have threatened and menaced myself with the denial of your obsession
I have studied the semaphore of your skin, see how it blazes and beckons
I have ripped down the boundaries of my senses to enclose the
        compass of your essence
I have sewn small bells to every bone to ring out my presence
I have launched myself into the inner orbits of your eyes
I have been excessively obscene, speaking in the lingo of soft drawn-out sighs
I have been assassinated by the bullets of ardor
I have raided the luscious sweetmeats in your larder
I have perched, a craved raven, on your shoulder
I have placed you in an immortal light so only I get older
I have taken on the physical form of the most rabid and indecent storm
I have collapsed comatose from aromatic inhalation at your door
I have tattooed frescoes of you over my body from neck to knee
I have sailed around your virgin shore on odysseys of depravity

And still I have been sentenced to silence by the court of your beauty
But I've made it my duty as your loyal and salacious slave
TO RANT ON ANYWAY!
Boy Abyss—your little delinquent ray of the flayed and delirious day

AS I ROAM THE HAREM OF MY HEAD

Adorned in magnificent swoon-plumes
She comes in her wanton wardrobe
And dips down through my skin
Into ecstasy zones among my bones

Entombed in this cathedral skull
Unsated among my spoils of greed
She strips down to her psychedelic scents
That bring the bludgeoned to their knees

And my eyes are studded
With blistered bliss
As she comes with conflagration fingertips
The ardor opiates—the rush, the hit
A single devastating kiss

She comes to feed the fetishes
From the Pantheon of the Unblemished
Evaporating lightly on my mouth
As all the lights of longing black out

And my eyes are jabbed
With slink splinters
As she comes as the Eternal Tease
With her fleshy fragrances on the breeze
A sigh-clone through my cinders

And she settles in my skeleton
As I roam the harem of my head
Wreathed in a halo of howling—
The benedictions of this bed

AMOROUS ARREST

She handcuffed him and read him his Fertility Rights

FAUNICATION OF THE FLOWERS

Orchid of Obscenity
Grow
From these seeds I sow
Lilly of Lust
Bloom
In the furrows of this room
Sunflower of Sin
Glow
In this fecund home
Tulip of Temptation
Flame
Burn away all shame
Violet of Vice
Rise
Before these eyes
Morning glory
Deflower
In this darkened hour

And in these flowers' names
Let it rain
Let it pour down
Upon this fertile ground

Lotus of Longing
Float
Your pale and scented boat
Magnolia of Moans
Unfold
The corolla of your clothes
Anemone of Ardours
Blaze
Carpet this glade where we lay

And in these flowers' names
Let it rain
Let it pour down
Upon this fertile ground

Let these flowers be strewn across the room

UNCONTROLLABLE INSTINCTS

I can not stop them leaping from the frenzy pool
I can not halt their scorching march through the lush lands
I can not control these creatures
They have never been tamed
So I am not to be blamed if they howl out your name

Instincts
Come ripping through my clothes
Instincts
Sharp needles to pierce stone
Instincts
My wanton weapons, my protecting pets
That swarm from ardor's ancestral nest

In my bed of bones they sleep in their immortal skins
Aeons they have slumbered within
Now they awaken and through my rib cage spring
These yelp-gatherers with their scented clubs
That run in havoc through the blood

Instincts
There is no leash to hold them
Instincts
They rise up on their flowering stem
Instincts
Out of the dark den into the light
To gnash, to snap and to bite

I am their king
And all my praises they sing
They are my riotous army
Who commit all my debased and unruly deeds
But trust me
I can not control these creatures
They have never been tamed
So I am not to be blamed if they howl out your name

I am not to be blamed if they howl out your name

DRAG ME AWAY

Drag me away
Drag me away
Drag me away
I will not struggle or resist
I was born for this
Drag me away
Drag me away
Drag me away
To your darkened cave
Keep me alive
On amorphous fruit
With luscious centers
And sticky juice
Drag me away
Drag me away
Drag me away
Make me a slave
Keep me trapped
Tortured on love
And the likes of that
Drag me away
Drag me away
Drag me away
This is the way to behave

THE IMMORTAL
RELIGION OF DESIRE

Gash me, gash me with light

How immortal you have grown
With your complete unadorned belief
O the Immortal Religion of Desire
Gash me, gash me with light
O the Immortal Religion of Desire
I will be one of your fold
I will believe in the most intimate of decrees
O the Immortal Religion of Desire
It is not too late in this desperate hour
O the Immortal Religion of Desire
See how these chains have fallen apart
And the scars have lifted from this heart
It is not to late in this desperate hour
O the Immortal Religion of Desire

Gash me, gash me with light

How immortal you have grown
With your mesmerizing acts of miraculous faith
O the Immortal Religion of Desire
Gash me, gash me with light
O the Immortal Religion of Desire
Destroy me, destroy me as I stand
Build me again with the perfect hand
O the Immortal Religion of Desire
I believe you can cure my most derelict disease
O the Immortal Religion of Desire
See how these cuts are ceasing to bleed
The hunger that now at last will feed
It is not too late in this desperate hour
O the Immortal Religion of Desire

Gash me, gash me with light

I who was blind, now have sight

HURLED AGAINST THE ADORABLE

The pleasure of the theft
The emotional core still left
I gather again my strength
No rest
No rest
Yes, yes, yes
Hurled against the adorable

The beauty of the crime
Such oblivion in your eyes
The softness of your breasts
Blessed
Blessed
Yes, yes, yes
Hurled against the adorable

The darkness feathers me
As I hover
I plummet, the hawk of a lover
Hurled by an unknown hand
Hurled against the adorable
Hurled against the adorable

The span of my arms
The radius of the whole world
I'm extinguished by a single breath
Unless
Unless
Yes, yes, yes
I'm hurled against the adorable

Hurled against the adorable

To break myself open

DRUNK ON THE DIVINE

You and your licentious elixir
I drank it in one gulp

Got any more?

SCRAWL OUT THE LAWS ON MY SKIN

Let abandon be my awakening
Let caution be my aching
Let release be my capture
Let giving be my rapture

Scrawl out these laws
On my skin
Cut them deep
Let them soak in
Let them soak in

Let devotion be my divinity
Let pleasure be my depravity
Let envy be my disaster
Let love be my master

Scrawl out these laws
On my skin
Cut them deep
Let them soak in
Let them soak in

Let the body be saturated
These are the laws I have created

Let them soak in

Let them soak in

PASSION DESIGNER

I ironed my double-breasted Seduction Suit to meet you
But now it's all crumpled

O WHOA, BABE INFERNOOOOOO!

Slink
In flesh pink
A halo's glow from the flow of larva beneath
Where I too sink to meet
All your molten men who still exist
In a magma of boiling bliss

And I see with a prophetic vision
I see it all with an anatomical precision
Mining the seams of your clothes
As you walk that wicked walk down the road

O whoa, Babe Infernoooooo!

Slink
As a cooling drink
For the ones with blistered lips
Flash your sabre hips
And as a woman warrior inflict your wounds
Seal us in our breathing tombs

Slink on—the road is long
Where I follow with my body
Hung with bells and gongs
Slink on—the path is narrow
Where I follow with a howling
Sounding through my marrow

O whoa, Babe Infernoooooo!

And I see you with such clarity
I see you in all your immaculate depravity
Mining the seams of your clothes
As you walk that wicked walk down the road

O whoa, Babe Infernoooooo!

Slink on—and in your dust
I will follow, a simple merchant
Trading chunks of life for nuggets of lust
Slink on—and in your wake
I will follow, as is my fate
Eternally reaching for the mirage I chase

O whoa, Babe Infernoooooo!

EXPOSED
TO THE NAKEDNESS OF THE WILL

I have torched myself
And stood before you
On fire
I have armed myself
With the sharpened weapons
Of desire
I have coated myself
In the invisible icings
Of love
I have feathered myself
And swooned down
As a delinquent dove

I am exposed
To the nakedness of the will
I am exposed
To the darts of every thrill

I have dyed myself
In the true colours
Of deliverance
I have placed myself
In the rites of a
Bodily trance
I have marked myself
With the crimson daub
Of a giant X
I have brought myself to you
A magnificent messenger
Of my sex

I am exposed
To the nakedness of the will
I am exposed
To the darts of every thrill
I am exposed...
So, before the wind blows and scatters me
Pluck the rose

MY CUSTOM, YOUR INSPECTION

I had to search so thoroughly
Before finding the small birthmark you smuggled

AAHHH!

You leapt into my life and stabbed me repeatedly with y' Ecstasy Knife

BEAUTY AND THE BITTEN

At your craft, you're the best
The way you tattoo your strange symmetries across my chest
Mystical messages, a heavenly code
The sign of the Ecstatically Blessed
Shining through my clothes

Obviously you're acquired
A taste for this
An addiction for my flesh
As you recite the litany beneath your breath
"This one's sweeter than the rest."

And I also find much pleasure
In being your living drug
As you come with your cravings to my table
And beg for the feast of love

Let your beauty bite me to the bone
And I, the Bitten, allow hunger to be written
In the language of exquisite moans

I lie down, a totem
On the floor of this room
Fully decorated with the flowers of my beautiful doom
My body, a beacon
Of dazzling jewels
The smear of your lips
With their crimson dew

I carry the seal of the Burning Beast
The emblem of Every Angelic Agony
The mark of the Great Debauched Disease
And the brands of all my ecstasies

Let your beauty bite me to the bone
And I, the Bitten, allow hunger to be written
In the language of exquisite moans

THE BOOK OF YOUR BODY

The book of your body
I furiously read
A pictographic script
Of a sacred creed
An open testament
To unabridged needs
A revelation of my own
Uncensored greed

And passing
These fingers over
The curves of your
Natural braille
It translates into
The intimacies
Of a vast seductive tale

The book of your body is in
All the present perfect tenses
Checked out for eternity
From the Library of the Singing Senses

An erotic thriller entitled:
THE ECSTASY EDICTS OF THE SWOON THRONE
A *Dictionary of Spangled Desires*
The Bible of Sighs and Moans
Chapters of unedited sexuality, radical depravity
Knotted tussles of lust, the unfathomable depths of love
The eternal fires of the forbidden
Surely the greatest book ever written

In present perfect tenses
Checked out for all eternity
From the Library of the Singing Senses

The book that I take to bed

Again and again it will be read

IN A CURVED MIRROR

She had polished her skin for him
So he stood there in front of her, reflected in her luminosity

RUDE AWAKENING

Her biological clock rang in her
Pronouncing the time of fuckundity

SMOLDERING WITH YOUR SCENT

I have your scent on me
It lingers on my skin
It penetrates further still
Entering my very bones within

It can't be washed away
The strength of the distillate never lessens
I bury my head in my hands
And breath in your pungent presence

I need to roll around, cover myself in you
Until quenched
I smolder with your scent

I smolder with your scent
It evaporates slowly as I lie
Overcome on the floor in spontaneous fire
As I close my eyes and sigh

I lick my bare arms along their length
I feed on you in every breath

I need to roll around, cover myself in you
Until quenched
I smolder with your scent

I smolder with your scent

THE RESURRECTION DANCE

Unleash your captive flight
Before my rabid appetite
Your body soaked in slithering rhythms
And bells of shrapnel light

O dance the Resurrection
To every flame unloosed
Dance the Resurrection
For sap rising in the shoot

Free me from behind
The bars of these eyes
An animal at once ignited
All at once deprived
And with my phantom mind
Now let me glide
Fastened to your curves
Sealed to your side

O dance the Resurrection
To the rekindled yelps of life
Being the shining saviour
Of all my crucified nights

SWEET-EYED CYCLOPS

Knowing he had a sweet tooth, she stretched out
And spooned sugar into the hollow of her navel

WHEN THE SERPENT SUCCUMBS TO TEMPTATION

Casting off his clothes
New devilry crept into her room

THE DARLIN' DARTS

I have 'em in me
I have 'em in me
Across my chest, down my neck
The darlin' darts
Are tipped with your intoxicating drug
Streaming through my blood
I have 'em in me
I have 'em in me

They can pierce all the armour I own
Rip through my clothes
Penetrate my soul
The darlin' darts
Are bristling in my side
I feel like some bleeding martyr shot through where I lie

Ah... thud!
They infect the blood
I've been delirious for days
In rigors of relentless cascades
I've had this ecstatic state, a blinding rush of bliss
I need you to kiss...

I need you to kiss my wounds
I need you to kiss my wounds

The darlin' darts
I have 'em in me
I have 'em in me
I'm impaled in their hail

O FABULOUS ALTAR

O Fabulous Altar, the sacrifice is prepared
Selected with care
By sinking to the knees in complicity

O Fabulous Altar, the sacrifice will lie
Before your eyes
So the nights can bleed with ceremony

Don't cut me down from your arms
Until the world turns to dust
Don't pull this heart from my chest
Until I've worshipped what I must

O Fabulous Altar
In my faith I will not falter
O Fabulous Altar
Lead me by the halter
Blinded by my faith
To your resting place

O Fabulous Altar, the sacrifice is bared
The feast to share
Take the holy knife to the remnants of my life

O Fabulous Altar, the sacrifice is cut
Its eyes are shut
Now to set fire to the long-awaiting pyre

Don't cut me down from your arms
Until the world turns to dust
Don't pull this heart from my chest
Until I've worshipped what I must

WOMAN OF THE PLAGUES

I have no immunity against you
All your beautiful diseases I am susceptible to

Thank goodness

A SPOON IT OUT

Aaa. . .
The spoon is in the jar
Where the blazing cherries are
Comes dripping
Dripping, dripping
Syrup on a spoon
The nectar of the moon

Spoon it out
Spoon it out

Spoon out the syrup, baby
It's running down the sides
Spoon out the syrup, baby
Manna for the blind

The spoon is held above
Piled with the fruits of love
Comes dripping
Dripping, dripping
O lay me down to swoon
Over a sticky spoon

Spoon it out, baby, spoon it out

Bury me in blazing cherries
Bury me in blazing cherries

I'm ready

PLUMED

I'm plumed with an urgency
A fountain of thirst
As a falcon with a tingling in its talons
Hovering over your earth

I'm overgrown with urges
A thorny thicket of instincts
And beneath my leather hood
I go blind with what I think

I'm plumed with a feathery flame
I'm plumed with a geyser of songs
Touch is magnified without eyes
A tincture of scent is strong

I perch in my obedience
Upon your wrist
And I will stay here for eternity
If that is your wish

I'm wide-eyed in my dark home
Vision-spears stab, I don't blink
And beneath my leather hood
I go blind with what I think

I'm plumed with a feathery flame
I'm plumed with a geyser of songs
Touch is magnified without eyes
A tincture of scent is strong

MAGNIFICENT METAMORPHOSIS

Unbuttoning your blouse you emerge
Soft white wings
Alighting around my neck

BOY ABYSS

He gave her his Oblivion Kiss that blacked her out

SEX PHOENIX,
FIREWATER'S DAUGHTER

Hey, here comes Firewater's daughter
Hey, here comes Firewater's daughter

I'm lust's long lost son, drunken and undone

O sex phoenix
How come her flames don't burn her?
I'm lust's long lost son
Under the spell of her fiery sermons

I've been baptised
By the bright infernos in her eyes
Charred and crucified
Thrown alive in the furnace of the burning bride

O sex phoenix
Again and again
You rise to the occasion
Again and again
I'm engulfed in the conflagration

Here she comes... Firewater's daughter
Risen again from the dead
Risen again from the dead
And so, into the flames we're lead

Pouring herself over me
Pouring herself over me
Pouring herself over me

Firewater's daughter is pouring herself over me

I'm lust's long lost son, lying here drunken and undone

THE WOLF IN MY WHISTLE

Standing on the corner with m' Howl Hat on
I let out a long wild inaudible whine as you pass

THE INDELIBLE EMBRACE

Although you're long gone
The imprint where you slept is still here on my shoulder

I'LL DRUM ON

The scented spices that you've painted down your thighs
Burn my tongue

I'm loosing the power of speech
Becoming nothing but a blazing human drum

This could be my last song

This is my last song

But I'll drum on

I'll drum on

from
THE YELP HOUSE KANTOS

One quick jab 'n' it is over, but the resonance continues a lifetime.

A MOTHER TO MILLIONS

In the beginning much is said and little done and vise-
versa, heads turning to see who is calling and stripping
down to their thoughts in public. The audience has
already left, but others come and clap, kissing without
paying. And you are born. But it never seems to stop you
playing the woman of the world, diving in the shallow
darkness, a mother to millions, with the whipping boys
jumping around drunk and timeless with rabid rhythm
and mating songs; a mass of hair coiling musically around
your body and back again. And the dim world in the scented
skimpy minutes after dark is biting again as the rush is on,
blindly heading there in our minds, the laughing inside
sweeping on to the shores: yours—lusty, plentiful, but secret,
a lump of sex like the drumboys rejoicing to be free, where
the hour comes and afterwards comes again, forever it seems,
until I know better than to ask. Now, amongst the twirly-
whirly districts a shimmering exhaustion runs or staggers home
and I have been whooping and step by step know the feeling,
the spanking-new fevers given every night where the call is
"Initiate and die, Wild Inebriates. Initiate and die"—in the
swoon-pools asplash, dipping in, and she talks of bliss and getting
away to where the world is quivering slowly with the Rhythm
and the Twisted, smoking their heads off baby, exactly burning
with precise flame. But by thunder they work, grappling, bar-
reeking, laying side by side. See, this stuff is good but blinding
and serene, knowing how to menace each capsized moment,
shouting and tattooing slowly with an undercurrent black and
slang. And we wade in, fighting a feverish war on all corners
in the seconds left on the road of a thousand darting natures,
heading on and away into the charming deaths and floating
idiotic lives, this blurred fuzzy-edged sanctum where we live.

COMING IN SOFT SKIN AROUND
THE CORNER IS ETERNITY
AND A FRIEND FOR YOU TOO

Come to bedlam with the torching and flashing Ms. Blade,
spiky and fun and blessed white heat. And coming down in
soft skin round the corner is eternity and a friend for you too,
young, eager, and a mess on the floor laughing, and you can't
find your clothes and your life for that matter and it is the
day of delirium to be not quite in the center of the bed,
senseless as she wants me to be that way; the drink making
us thirsty for other things, the crashing around in the light,
the old bombardment up to its tricks again. Tonight the song
is ripped up and scattered and we love to hear it this way,
caught in the act and a difficult one to follow, up the tiny aisles
leadened with stars, appealing but not as dangerous as where
the hour stains deepest and wishes outlive promises ten to one.
And when frenzy is calm and comforting a lot of praise and glory
has gone into it, packing it with the slices of life we want
to keep together in a constant explosion and hundreds of other
blissful encounters in the frothy mess. O, you look so devilish in
your horned-hat and the burning ponytails and the clothes and
fingers that have seen sin on the top floor and codes of kissing.
But I walk through many of the finer points before reaching
the rough and courser languages, undone and waiting. Here
the old sexguitar birdboy song is an anthem, filtering down from
rarefied air. "No more of it," you keep saying but we plough on.
The streets lay here and there, untouched with the appearance of
being utterly mauled. Of course this can't be true—those here are
gentle sorts, noted for blowing single plain emotions up into the vast nights.
See, here one comes now.

100

IT IS TIME TO STRIKE OUT
FOR OTHER SEXPOTS

One day I will settle down to a world of frenzied
intention and unjustified ogling. But now the action is
thickly spread, swerving to this side and that. Pretty.
It is viscous. So never trust the fully clothed with their
giant morals dripping from their chins and the fluted
whooping taking short-cuts through the inane aisle,
sleeping and blundering on in rapt inattention.
You won't believe this, but the trick is clever enough
to be an everlasting source for the hypnotic, springing
delightfully flesh-shaped out of Yelp Street where:
"How can you be indifferent when the Splash covers and
drenches every principle-in-the-book and your adorned
cheeks, kiss-marks, and black unfathomable symbols do
wonders for the complexion?" Ho! Away in a mood
among the ruins, propelled by fidgety enthusiasm into
events you haven't seen and find inescapably dangerous.
This is all foreseen. The accolades, the Pose of Triumph
rearing up and perched in splendor, then a quick grab,
a squeal, and the men and women don't know right from
banging heads together and those squabbling in ecstasies.
So who to believe? Who to pour over? What complicity?
Alone with the Wearing and Tearing, the useless moments
strung around you, the sensual souvenirs lying tossed
and panting over the covers, it is time to strike out for
other sexpots with that airy look-of-the-last-living-
disturbance. Frazzled, waving, miraculous somersaults.
I will show them.

COOL CATECHISMS ON THE HILL

I am a natural drum, I enter thrashing.

Standing with language, explosive, a delinquent vibrancy,
my songs are recited as cool catechisms on the hill.
The walk is infinite but I am thank goodness immortal—
cutting across the exotic lawns and rivers in camouflaged
dresses, the scent of syllables on the wind, the traps set,
mouths open into the future. True, I go by many names:
"The Thirsting Rhythm Reader Among the Yelping,"
"The Drumhatter," "The Pose of Dictum Unto Squeals,"
but someone must live this way. The portable images are
carried in and placed perfectly with the scant cooing and
the trim thinking. My reasoning goes like this: the mute
slip off the page so easily, only the great Human Drums
beat on. They are remembered, scored to music blasts.
It is a mammoth undertaking, but I feel better. For this is
how dark I pierce, how wanton I allow my language to
proclaim the Night of Sexual Sorcery open to the pretty
public (and only the pretty). There is movement within
the dappled phrases. No need to be nervous. Fear is
ravaging another beauty and ignoring you and the
dressing-up begins by stripping down. It is costly, of course,
but each soul is raised, and the fun with the musty belief
always outlives the lit one. The torturing goes on in pleasant
surroundings and the silence is deathly alive.

RUSHING FROM ONE
FIREHOUSE TO ANOTHER

"Come to bedlam," you whisper, "without scruples,
you pet, loaded with gifts, flesh-mur and a body
embroidered with sexual stories with the dark parked
on your curves." And so missing every other word
of my rattling song you know me better than anyone,
sifting out the relevant and the succulent, dashing
through the hole to grab the babies stripped of their
principles and here is danger's daughters saying and
doing whatever they want. So once reality is ratified
for good we'll feel better, crashing around on these
young legs with ambitions blocking the runways of
our flight. So lovers, take up your positions, lewd in
the evening air. And the smoke above our heads
signaling how we lie in bed for hours motionless and
Wham Blam and the Runaways and the sheepish
goddess all naked and Oblivion himself with his dark
circles and lovable theme songs rushing from one
firehouse to another. Now the virgin hour enters and
is stunning, colorful among the old shadows, skirt
lifted and traveling fast. And this time the present will
get the better of us, streaming from our necks and
ankles, the music always coming first, words mincing
in for a nice chat in sloppy sweaters and fierce nudity.
And I read the faces tossing around in wild bedrooms
as the night is remembered through time to where the
precious seconds are yours and useless and almost
forever. So instead there is dance hunger, the new
wheels turning and you and I forging human shapes
with curling eyelashes.

BURNING IN THE ELOQUENT
SILENCE OF MUTE GREATNESS

The sky in our throats, the mottoes lit up ahead.
I pass out for years and minutes later on knees
and elbows charge through the door.
You say, "I'm liable to do anything in this state,"
gently massaging my dangerous years. And so you hoodwink at me
and stand burning in the eloquent silence of mute greatness,
not a limp in your language
but perfect love in the time and tales of unrest.

SO YOU SAY, SLOWLY POURING OVER ME

So wait by the entrance and exit with me to the sleepden.
And we come flying through the mist, dusks and dawns
ripening, cantering in our flimsy high points of life,
existing outstretched and daring. Are we out to impress
with our sickly colors and the blue and browns of our
eyes? Not this time. We move closer to the scents and
emotions that are feeding us. You implore, ripping back
the sheets, staring at the ceiling: "Here are the angels,
buxom and beating their wings." So you say.
So you say, slowly pouring over me.

THE INEBRIATED MINUTE

The inherent diseases pass from one thought to another
until they are hummed like blind infectious melodies and
the tidal darkness covers the anthem. But we amble on.
I, reading the riot act (every page). You, Babe Sugarcane,
singing your famous "The Ultimate Idol and Penultimate Idiot" song.
The swoon sisters are as jealous as hell: collapsing, beautiful garbage.
And you can't beat that! For when a passionate life exists,
the inebriated minute is worth its weight in fire.

YOU KNOW HOW TO DRINK
YOUR BRILLIANT FURY

Babe? (Can I call you that?) May I lick your fingers?
Slowly, so very slowly, when you emerge naked
you know how to drink your brilliant fury—
a dance I have watched you execute.
And at times you have no pity for dances.
They are to be made senseless—
the trashing, asking the night its limit: tribal, volcanic.
O Darling Slaughter, let me brand you with whispers.

ONE CRACK-POT NOTION
DELIBERATING OVER ANOTHER

Now I will describe the feeling, the gray part, the bright
florid pieces, the vast headdress piercing the night, the
wailing blades. Much of the time the music is the
supreme complicity acting as a shadow, the dark arias
dripping down the V-dress, plunging to the drum-shaped
heart. "Unnoticed, the minor sensual phrases become the
world's sexual slogans." This is how you seem to put it:
demonstrative and purring. But what next? Dark ravages
are best taken under mild delirium; emotional roots
crowning, topping the night, eyes knifish, a life of
abandon in front. The splash-dictum is leaking, trickling
down the body to the wells of knowledge, worldly
frenzy and human-bloodcurdling. And again the limping
will not subside, skies become lopsided, with
one crack-pot notion deliberating over another.

BLAZING LOVE BITING GOING AROUND

Each girl's hair tied with fiery insanity,
blazing love biting going around, plucked thoughts,
crushing silence, magnificent screams. Moreover,
the lines leading to blinding vistas are whipping
through the darkness, the singer pronouncing each
part of the lyrics with sodden lucidity, the hum-
anthem on our lips. And once awake, the enriching
fevers, the unclassified emotions pelt each skin. Lie
down, endure. How wonderful to find the labels torn
out but the dress fits after years of shimmering
dancing and terrifying thoughts. The calm is stormy
but weatherable and how little we have changed with
our peaked eyebrows, wanton tongue-twisting
vowels, the sensual object dance; the long awaiting of
childhood instantly cured, streets crackling, yapping
as I bring the exotic-look, the braided longing
like a drug. Thirsty, desperate, spinning in the
contagious nature of the scents delivered in the dark
clubs, the voice is clear, revelationary, broken and
spiced and given out. The races continue around me,
all winning in their own miniature ways, denying the
eternal in the slow plod, the death-spooking.
I am battered in fierce colors, as I lunge and run,
run and lunge in the quarters, the kissing habitat;
the grunt-girls quietly wearing their tremulous clothes.
And once time has been peeled it dries and withers.
I make moisture in the eyes and eat the mortal menu;
the whirling hymns of the lacerating passions an
ineluctable event. But I must wait, cocked as an
unabridged language in the beautiful views through
the cracks, the mouth sealed with glutinous dye.

I WEAR BURNING FINGERTIPS, UNSETTLING EYES

The journey takes place in small circles dotted with
light and unknown corners but familiar as if lived in a
series of sideways glances and flowering memories
until it lies dormant under a covering of parsimonious
theatrics. I grasp it, barbed and bristling with the
same-old-story-in-a-different-order. I wear burning
fingertips, unsettling eyes. It is not what is "in" the
experience but what comes "out" of it: the line of
fire camps we run to, one after another, the ruffled
voices, the squealing that must be ignored. Now I am
inert, the dipping of the tongue in the Nightjar
allowing autonomous life to twitch and slap-dance
through the baited aisles, babe. I thrust into this,
following the scents of sound like little killjoys,
hailing the rumble-souls so naked that the night has no
cover. But songs like this come only every century or
so and even not recognized then. I pour in and out of
the one placed here. The origin and the destination
have disappeared but the ideas move. Forthwith it will
be dark, sniff it babe, enjoy it. Tense for a second I
come bursting out, a natural safeguard for the mad
wink and the frenzy perched on the headdress.
But the laying down and waiting will pass.
The ceiling entering the sky, decanting beauty from
this body to that, calling it "wonderment" but knowing
it is only a phase of youth walking away.

STAY AWHILE, A LIFETIME OR TWO

In the quiet hours we get ready, preening, resting.
The lolling, an opulent, dewy surrender to succulence.
The peace is unparalleled at a glance but luckily
unsustainable. I don't want this. I bet on flaying
nightfuls, jangling mouthfuls, the Great Daub being
the hullabaloo, being the fling into this sea.
So I will climb up and catch this world shattering all
expectations, a breathlessness that can not be got over,
a pearly enamored second where I wear the honorific
eyepatches and the slurring whistle and where the first
stop is you, untangling your sex songs. "Stay awhile,
a lifetime or two." "Perhaps later." All the rigmarole is
enchanting, crowing in the evening. Though a living
must be made from mild delinquent beckoning, studying
the clip-clop of your feet, the conscious portrait of one
aware of immense sensual power. But ripening is
constant, infinite, and I feel it in my body, not aging
but ripening. The premeditated whoops are arranged in
immortal strategies to lead her by trails of sugared-lingo
into this house—the one with the pink walls and gruesome
decor. Talk is decreased to the fragments given to mean
anything, interpretations not translations, and as a story
of intrigue it works well. See, isn't it more exciting to be
misunderstood in the emotional realms of intensity? Yes.
Other movements, other courses along the river are riding
about seeking impressions, stenciled shadows over the
bed. But no one teaches life—it is to be passed around,
never challenged; for it is this that fits us out in our fiery
faces, the dimpled cheeks and the gem-studded
eyebrows. Against the shouting matches a rare saturation
of top-billed moments take shape, tossing their hair,
looking daring and erotic and quite immortal in the
middle of the day. Huh!

AFTER THE WAVE
OF BROKEN LIP SERVICE

I adore these moments
after the wave of broken lip service and crumpled love
has passed over and been swept into a pile
of clutter on the corner of our lives.
Sorted they seem innocent enough,
jammed together they are a brilliant rage
flopping this way and that.

THE BRUISED NIGHT

Ah, penetrating, that look! Another world carried away
in the thick emotions up to our knees.
Plodding around I find a renewed interest in the Bruised Night.
It is like theater but more unleashed. Words slapped down.
Here the bed is not the central object.
The tasseled ears, dyed wrists, splattered lugubrious songs
mince in and out. I look at you.
You are exploring a vast floor of memories where I am uninvited.

THE DICTIONARY OF MY SCRAPES AND FROLICS

I live out of bounds with a bell around my neck.
I can be reached at certain times in certain places, night-hopping.
When the Dictionary of my Scrapes and Frolics becomes a best-seller
there will be jumbled interviews that cannot be pieced together.
These are the secrets you whispered that time, the ones I crossed my
heart and hoped to live for. I am bandaged.
After a while the thoughts don't hurt.
They go away and you pass by—your feathered dress all of a flutter.
Silence crumbling, I tear up my clothes and start again.

MAKING LIFE WITH THE LIGHTS ON

I am a natural drum. I enter thrashing.

I look down on what is smashed, select the deafening
pieces and build a great mute language. The house is
scattered and I am making life with the lights on.
Mostly it is skew-wiff but it fits. I walk in style,
the years in torrents, flapping like flags from my
shoulders. But we are still recognizable: the same old
colorful tongue-pulling, the same old darkened grace.
The rave reviews are pouring in. We read them as the
plot thins and we arrive in the night in pairs, perfectly
united and identical. You, brazen and flaunting your free
will. I, headstrong, and at times wanting to be that
flaming dagger stared at in the acrobatic whistle-aisles.
There is hair-combing and lip-brushing but above all
these layers there are blackeyes and scuffling.
Religion from life streaming out on its way home.

UNFATHOMABLE BEGINNINGS AND ENDS

Fine. It can be taken as it stands or lays down.
Or it can be kept in the corner of the eye as a constant
source of devilry and fun; and furious writing wades
around exploring the seedy clubs with its air of
detachment and ruminative glazed look.
The unforgettable face in its many reflections is smoking
and blowing twinkling imaginations in our direction.
This is nothing unusual. Just tear out this piece and
plaster it up in the room, smothered with other gripping
and sensational news. It is not the melodious that we sing
along to but the sawing voice-like ratchet of a musical
instrument infinitely making a cathedral of hums through
us. Then I rejoice. Then I give praise. This nameless
litany is a girl with her hair tied back with burning wire,
a cavalcade settling poison on us, whisking the true days
away and replacing them with unfathomable beginnings
and ends. So I've been told.

START AGAIN AND RETRACE YOUR STEPS, SENSELESS THING

Start again and retrace your steps, Senseless Thing.
You who I have just met emerging in a sprawling beauty.
The kicking is by bullies and in this age all my stroking
makes you edgy. Crash! I'm right. The poetic evening is
in trouble, and the wearing of trinkets and flirty quiffs
will be historic, remembered, forgotten, and goggled at
by the audience, agog with crackling sleeplessness.
The power is in buckshot looks, the dipping in the pools
built for imaginary forays, cool, neverlandish. I wear
the cap given me by the Naked Fever Girl with the
Thunderclapping Drum. It's how I peak, ripping up
unnecessary maps and ground-plans that are tricky and
deceptive little beasts. Cheerleading is at least arousing,
leg-high and a way to keep ideas boiling. Off I go,
chunks and slices of rhythm under me, the lights dim,
the stage will shock you in low-cut panoramas although
there are some bodies you can not watch. They are illicit
and forbidden and worth more than the riches scooped up
through the years and spent with a gush. Ha! The flame-
seeking is one excitement. I have reserved the most
brilliant moments of this life in the corner for two.
We are ravenous. Gulp after gulp of elixirs as we laud
the performance—the strapless fur visions smeared in
beauty-juice and smiling—they drape the chairs and once
you get over the embarrassment, the syrup-dancing is
aflow and the talk thickens. "I didn't tell you how fat
and delicious love became. The evening is darkening but
there is time to eat, gouge ourselves silly."
And afterwards? Afterwards is something very human,
an indescribable journey between huge generation gaps,
sumptuous centuries and the occasional chill ruffling the
hair. This is why determination is a coat-in-arms.
So relax into the immortal mannerisms, the way your hand
is upon me, the rings seamless rosettes sparkling.

KING CHANGE

This is the magical second that was presumed dead or existing in a musty side winding. It comes flying, settling like a genius at our feet. Something this precious cannot be owned, but the squabbles turn over topsy-turvy, and you wish the long volatile night would dawn or grow infinitely drunker. It does. Both. Yet it is hard to tell. It slams closed. The ceiling is painted with swirling eroticisms, stiff and brittle and not coated with those feelings you and I have been wearing throughout the evening. Hauled in, the music overwhelms and nothing is left that is prim and proper. Grasping the meaning is only the tip, the sheet of knowledge that is suddenly ripped back exposing your body. I haven't read it before although the experience after experience is vaguely familiar but tinglingly new. This one, braying with its flutey plume, is the greatest. King Change with the studded neck is lovable and tangle-haired, and I talk of his voyages, the ones I take to the other side of Desperate Measures and the Silhouette That Storms the Birthclub. Then swing, carve a niche, and the shimmering carnival passes with its glittering clothes, dull in comparison with the highlights and wild whistling emitting from the dark center. It is this that I will have the first dance with, sweeping me off my feet. I whisper, "I will be the Raging Sway, the Leader." This language is to be followed to the word, to be buried in belief, tasseled in a mass of jargon, a mumbling hymn and phrases splashing the street back from the dead and smothered with praises and arm-raising, and we see light and hug, ideas soaked in new relevance.

TO CRY OVER WORDS
IS A RARE PRIVILEGE

It was spectacular, showering and splintering emotions,
gesticulating and explaining the finer movements until
they were exhausted, baffling but worth watching, the
rich embroidered colors cracking open and the softer
sex collapsing in an induced frenzy on the sidelines.
How tired I have become, drained by an almighty
yanking from the floor in tufts. But to cry over words is
a rare privilege given only to the few. A gift,
an immeasurable flying, elation, with the horned hat
donned in one sacred flash through the bewildering
whackrooms. The singers understand their throats,
wrapped in killer instincts, performing duty after duty
to the ears; the sound beyond suffering; the jutting
breasts, the plain serene glares penetrating clothes with
unutterable sentences, everything busying itself with a
vigor that is a ritual, shaking out the songs from their
boxes, the universal girl walking through the crowds
with the mutable features streaming before and behind.
Here she sits, destroying and building, and it is slowly
recognized as the same flame-waving and most delicate,
and coming from somewhere without thinking, brilliantly
colored and astounding with the diving in and out of the
Thrive, alive in small doses but flat and endless on a
worldly scale. I grab what is offered, lie in the scent,
feeling a great depravity dancing in the potent powwow.

I AM A SPLINTERING MASS
OF THE ALL HUMAN

Now I'm going to tell you rich anecdotes lined with sex
and as much spluttering as can be loaded and spat out.
Once stories are poisoned they eternally pass from mouth
to ear and all this is not about rummaging but being
startled aghast that makes the juices drip, the fever revel,
the pungency of the odd thought open out. I am the new
door. I am a splintering mass of the All Human. I am
worth it. I am irrelevant. Why can't all this be taken for
granted? Give up crawling. Take up long erratic leaps
and lolloping, baby, in make-up and smeared with glitz.
Now there are punch-up and curses. Let us go cheap,
a repetition of oversized reasons that add up to "I will
always find you beautiful. Immensely so." Not many
words can say that. Not much honesty either. Much has
been cluttered with chunks of the Impetuous Instant,
confessions steaming up your angel-winged glasses
when the tingling becomes so shrill, branding my name
between those nipples, the dilapidated women running
and touching, with wails, hoots, and ahs. I have it down
pat. Once you've mastered the wink, we, the Incendiary
Twins, icy, chiseled and pleated are adored. Our battle
cries twist serpentine in and out, emotional wisdom
drugged, enjoying every second of it with a limp, with a
s-stutter, collapsing in a fantastic heap. One young bell
will sway this thickheadedness, and one unique
phenomenon is the same as the next, the bustling and
rummaging in the bottom of the drummer heart until the
hinges are off you, havoc-smile, viperous eyelids.
A screech of love and I hop in. Slam. Garments tossed;
the years we are knotted in are deplorable and muffled up
with swoon-lined coats. The iron snarl peering out, the
natural impulses remedying the dizzy climate that pours

out of one sky into another, as if we were safe, chosen to
eat the Starving Tom Tom, as the noises come under the
door. For those that were once ignored, prove essential
to the melody. See darling, listen as the nights swing into
action although occasionally I'd like to be out of touch,
supine and dream-mouthed. Fat chance.

OUR NAKED·RUN-AMOK SELVES

Slowly Babe Sugarcane, we seem to be drifting apart,
flooring each other with walloping punches. What a sham.
I go on bewildering forays, furnishing these tales with
subject matter choked in clawing aberrations and whims
skipping on ahead. Filled with Beating Intoxicants I cannot walk a straight line. The homeward path is a grapple,
attractions twinkling and luring with an imperceptible
grace. On the sly we place our disguises together.
There is Greatness in this Unknown. But please don't
recognize me. Let's act the half-wits, smoldering topknots
and long wistful ideals. How calm it is. Our lives
evaporating inch by inch in these hands—these I write
with. The exhilaration of the Night Ploughing speaking
through the wild wrists, the Flap Dance that bursts in and
discovers you high and riding with the best. The plain facts
recede, leaving a stack of unrequited information falling
around our ears, our naked run-amok selves.

EXHAUSTION HILL

Come to bedlam, babe, slung in weepy colors,
the choral fireplace stoked and screaming. There is new
ground to be trod in a wealth of emotional bandages, unique
timing, riveting motifs across our chests; being as casual as
we can in this melee, arbitrarily edged in sultry meanings and
hollow consequences, a racy bumbfoundedness cracks
everyone up. Now the days unfold briskly. There is no time
like this one. Nothing to relive but step on and quash instead,
lick fingers, and rave about the finishing touches. Early to rise,
lingering over the absurd notion that this plain sailing is
endlessly running aground in the blackened buildings,
with spirals of smoke waking us in the middle of our
apoplectic mutterings. Ideas are reversed, crashed into one
another and these soft words beat our bodies into submission.
Torn up, prickly, drippy eyes exuding the faint twinkle-vanity
and slaughter to jump the Exhaustion Hill with the Prod
Dance, all are voluptuous, with cleavages dropping in with
that unabashed distorted beauty and kissing full on.
But nothing waits that long. It goes on and on, cantering and
flaying. The results are exhilarating, stretched out bare. I will
it. Busying myself with short dresses, freezing desires pulped
but unfolding in a torrent. And this hat will do. Trussed,
feisty, mewing, I will rake the shouts together so this hearing
tinkles the ear-rings, them swaying, them my tassels,
red-gushed in the most steamy way.

CASCADING THROUGH UTTER TRAVESTY

Suddenly I make my move, not with the blatant eyesores
tidying their lushrooms for business but with the crisp
unearthly prattle I want in spinning wimpy halos. Now is
the test, the writhing they do for attention, competing for
the best artistic plummets into the dark accolades with no
clothes in sight. Just lie here. The jumble of events is
passing by, freshly derelict with the pinions out. And so
we are cascading through utter travesty, a salute here and
there to acknowledge how we will brave the void traps
that yawn for the tired. Up! Take none of this. There is a
range of listless depravities awaiting each and every one
of us, the sulky, almost tipsy, jeweled personae, slipping
on convention, and I too will sprawl at different feet until
I am caught red-handed. Nabbed with subtle wording
written right across the breasts. It is the reversal quota,
like a swagger minus the accompanying foul-tongue
equaling a mad epidemic spreading over this night,
infectious to the touch of every burgeoned emotion that is
advertised as "The Tallest Order of the Day", that won't
sit still for even one single lifetime, I ask you. Laugh,
entwining full enjoyment up with irrelevant nitpicking, a
social evaluation, pompous in airy, always flaky,
attitudes sinks above it in thick cuckold divinity;
askance but with questions so elite that they shoot over
the head to become embedded in the interiors around
ourselves. Ho! The pace refuses to lose its urgency.
It is spurred on when you and the others use your
evaporating skill to pilfer ideals, where the audacious climaxes
level off in a sustained pitch, and the baring of what
was once covered is now a ritual that is quite natural, a way
of life, a way of death, sacrificing nothing of the
narrowness we step in or the clinging fanaticism kept
secret, but surfaces as a massive overdose of longing
complacency, strolling around till a whiff of spiritual
help drags us in. Sit here astounded. I do. Will always
do. The inhabitants here seem to know only chinks of

themselves, caught in the woo-woo currents. Tell me
what is endurable and what isn't! I can make decisions
and chop things up. That's easy. Harder is the value
placed on the Loyal Aberrations in the Kinship Snare.
I have been doing this for years and years and years.
There are no rules but those that constantly change
(I must subsist this way), adding an "O" to the grand
multitude of ornaments, so rays burst out, so I sweep the
whole length of the streets in a weaved slut-suit, with the
ever-ready backfiring trumpet bleating, the monumental
plunder from the sumptuous archives and the deformed
beautifications that will wrangle for attention when they
slim down and flutter their large sexual strategies in front
of whatever moves.

A MAJOR RAPTUROUS POSITION

Waiting in a major rapturous position, gashed make-up,
streaming delusions, the spill of these laughable quotes
going asunder, nose-diving with the firm belief that
hunger is always fed, light will open the shutters, the
debris will be hurled through the sky and ha, I will glow
with reason. There is perfection on its way, rallied in the
Squeeze Rooms. The genius of the alphabet, sodden with
meaning, spells out the rebellious, the whack-tunes in a
jumble in my arms; pieces all of a-litter. And here comes
the fanatical revelations as the reading adds up and I
crumble into existence. You can't say this without
conviction, without riots streaming through the blood,
peppering resistance in a rat-a-ta-tat, with the ravages
disappearing and luxuriating in forms of weird bliss
and unpunctuated highlights flashing and getting to grips.
Now it is clear-headed, mussy. The stumbling is a
unique preparation for the long-awaited naked youth
shivering, a grasp so spontaneous it ignites, starting with
the sharp fingernails scrawling your name. Quite aimless
are the tantalizing all-absorbing Acts of the Frivolous
gyrating in front of your wild-nimble presence. But frolic
on, King Blather, in the tamed rooms, a consortium of
unruly feelings causing the night to slosh into the day,
the upheavals to be touted in the streets, and the obscene
images to be quashed where they stand. There is nothing
better than the route twisted and wound up in yourself.
Patches of wide open gore take on pleasant symmetry,
assumptions are tackled, and I fall in beside your desire,
splattered with the creeping canons vanishing. For to
wheedle into the sheer catastrophes is to discover the
explosive dances thrown out of the wishy-washy club.

THE BLAND, THE DUMB,
AND THE PRETTY SENSELESS

Rupture and spew it all over the room. Lie down with the eternal
dialogues between the "selves," the big bad babble smashing in the
door, and rhetoric, with that dumb look sounding off with every
opinion worth ignoring. For this is how conversation works, the
drab and the bright colors matching, the silence saying nothing.
Your rhythmical bickering is indecipherable when it is
angry, although I see through it to the slow beat at the
cryptic core and I cuddle the great wound that others have
either neglected or made and we become the reciprocal
poultice lying over each other, shields in a nuptial frenetic
union. Of course, the mighty job of imprinting my
viewpoints on your lives is small now you think, with little
derisive eyes and weighty shrugs. But the spawning
season is long, unappreciated for its insanely mannered
inflections, the odd twitch of a single word, the escalating
wrath of meditation, the innate power screwed in so tight,
and the hoarse reasons blazing the trails as you drink
what was once the bland, the dumb, and the pretty senseless.

THE RAVISHING DOCTRINES OF THE AGE

Time is filled with sickly episodes, stylized in a sluggish
assault that pours out, as the scramble turns on me with
an entirely hypothetical affection. In the end everything
wriggles out of its own erosive powers and no kiss is
that diluted, concentrating on the twin threats: Beautifully
Tailored Tolerance and the Equally Gorged Flattery that
rank their proud and highbrow presence among the
ravishing doctrines of the Age. Arms up and feet
splayed, heat-robes creased, the epics aisles where we
have groveled-at-will, the noises that increase to the
limits, a soaked cavalcade of censored and smudged
litigations, disown life in a steamy enfolding parody
or in a ragged or exposed or squelched estheticism.
So the ideals hemorrhage and seem better for it, the
night-eating tucking in to engulf a precious incorporeal
reverence; the young exotics in jerky-styles writing their
breviaries: "What is conquerable now?" The humdrum
spheres are gnawed and spindly. Better to plump up the
culture to its expanded girth; the deep gorges flattening
out over the smooth thigh-reaches, where there is
skin-dipping for the Enlightened and tossed around half-
life lived to the full—all thoughtlessly prepared
with sweet punches and a great unconscious deliberation.

NEW OBJECTS OF ECSTASY

Thank you for being obtuse, wreathed in indistinct
visions that grovel lovingly, making up for lost time
in the chaotic pastures. I'll tell y', thank you for being
inflammatory in doses above the quotients of Natural
Occupancy. This is the heraldry written across you in
the greatest letters as I read to the literate. But the sounds
will not own up to their new slants on the masterly
Anthems of Amour or the harassment they get for not
slotting into their lingual mush-houses. It is necessary
to completely alter the course of a language, slap it with
an "implicit" sticker, wean it off nice crisp eloquence
onto things of the jagged larynx, babe. Wallowing in a
stupendous cleavage of swaddled epics and glistening
whinnies. We take no antecedents, stuffing the pompous
with their own snappy derelictions. Don't be squeamish!
The realism is never squandered by fabricating lines of
fashionable attire. It is completely abandoned and
new objects of ecstasy are picked out of the yelp hat.

from
THE 88 INTENSITIES
A Book of Charms

THE SHRAPNEL OF EACH SECOND

Boy Abyss *is the sage of the raw ruckus of the day, speaking in the penetrating shrapnel of each second; singing amongst the orgies of energy that inhabit the orbits of the living arena. At the onset of this transcription, his voice was disguised as randomised roars and assorted discord that I presumed to be the city's pulsing bloodstream. I was a mere vessel that received the sacrament of the tongues, and the charms appeared with little warning as to their plan or their potency. Only now do I realise that I obviously had aspirations to be a Rumble King, to twist the veins into a divine fuse, to bathe in an unearthly existence among the transmutable taboos, and to grow mighty crests of seduction on my arid forehead. I thus found myself receiving the pronouncements of a visceral orator. Boy Abyss recited the trigrams and I became the dutiful scribe of his office.*

THE 88 INTENSITIES are fully charged as their name implies— charged with the emissions of the cytoplasmic churnings of a vast city; irradiated with a vibrant force. Each charm reflects an experience, an instant where I stood and inherited the anointment of the streets, the blessings of the great flux around me. And in this triggered state, the charms have a magnitude, an instability as has uranium but also an explosively giving nature. Their stored vitality can be mined.

The charms provide an exile far from home. For those who seek to recover the elapsed aeons from the blood briars; for those who wish to hold the prized panacea of invisibility; for those who desire to go where the Bliss Babes are mating, then here are territories to traverse. Live out the instructions; do as is directed. Compliance allows the charms to provide their succor, to imbue the partaker with a sense of the astounding, to furnish a glimpse of realms yonder. Within them lies an exercise in energies; exploratory journeys through the concavities and convexities of a lush wilderness; a way to disturb dimensions, to plunge obliviously beneath the surface of the known.

In Japanese mythology eighty eight is a number of great significance. The ideogram for rice—the sustenance of the soul—is crafted from it. Reaching the heights of this age is celebrated as one of the principle nodes of longevity on the Buddhist calendar.

1.

TO ATTAIN THE STATUS OF A RUMBLE KING

(i)

Twist Damned Thyme and Doom Thistles into your crowning topknot
as emblems of your emphatic authority.

(ii)

Jab in the Eclipse Drugs and ascend gracefully into your own wanton orbit.

(iii)

Unleash legendary acts of providence by engulfing the Empirical Fire,
by slaughtering the Spineless Hour—
acts to keep the minions under your mesmerism.

6.

TO BE AN ADEPT READER OF THE RAMPAGES

(i)

Disguise yourself as a Mire Warrior dressed in knuckle plumage
and go on the Roar Path among the Imbecilic Isles spinning blather tales of yore.

(ii)

Let out a sperm wail.

(iii)

Squirm your way into the elite Snarl Spangled Depredation Den
by dropping the names of the devastated.

16.

TO CARVE THE GREAT PEAKS INTO FAMILIAR PILLARS OF OBEDIENCE

(i)

Hey, Flesh Wedge, there's an antidote in your determination
to rival the elementary order.
Brandish your blizzard-daubed mace in a menacing enactment.

(ii)

Dance your steamy and spectacular fling
without heed for the hostile editors of erotics
or the judgments pronounced by the stern.

(iii)

All your scars are the strokes that complete the grand corporeal talisman.
Lay out your wounds.

17.

TO CONJURE THE EMBERS
INTO THE LEGIBILITY OF INFERNAL DESIRES

(i)

There are soul-snappers to wrestle to the depths of blood squalls,
rile-piles to clamber up.
Go among the allergic, spreading the gospel according to Rejuvenating Lunges.

(ii)

Spit light into the face of the insidious Bruise Boys.

(iii)

Jack up a great dose of jugular plumes to smooth your rumpled journey,
to calm your besieged frailty.

18.

TO TEACH THE HERMETIC JINGLES
TO THE DISCIPLES

(i)

Wearing your bell-sporran, bob to your visceral beat.

(ii)

Use your little mating yelps with their addictive echoes
to attract the throng to the feeding trough.

(iii)

Know that your auspicious instrument is broken
but your compositions are unaltered.

20.

TO BE A SUCCESSFUL BLOOD-HOWLER

(i)

Be a lock unto your own anarchy.

(ii)

Awaken the entire havoc-combed reef of your neighbourhood
with the hum of the Hymns of Popular Abomination.

(iii)

Tattoo yourself with targets that are iridescent in the dark aisles
and walk with majestic vulnerability through the charged atmosphere.

26.

TO PASS UNRECOGNISED THROUGH
THE DOORWAY TO ILLICIT ECSTASIES

(i)

As you knock, shield your clamorous urges with an unruffled carapace.

(ii)

The Interstices of Order are stoically glinting up ahead.
Go fill them with your back-handed blather, Boy Reel.

(iii)

Smear on your glossy rascal rouge, line your eyes with urge-antimony,
and be ushered in as the Great Carved Pariah of Depravation.

41.

TO IMPRINT THE REVERIES OF THE EVENING FROLIC VESTIBULE ON A VIRGIN COUNTENANCE

(i)

Sit among the Slur Weavers and learn how to piece together
the parables of their relics.

(ii)

Finish off the Flayday by wandering with your shirt open to the imbecilic ends.

(iii)

The Street of Exuding Ardors is loaded with a startling fecundity.
Awaken from your dormancy.

43.

TO BE LOOKED UPON AS THE ANOINTING BENEFACTOR
OF THE PARCHED

(i)

Lick your swoon-spoon with a rabid abandonment.

(ii)

Skewered in the Rude View, remain an absolute rippleless sheen of the spirit.

(iii)

Sprinkle your jewelled fertility over the Agog and reap the growth of your farming.

44.

TO THRIVE IN AN ALL-IMMERSED EXILE
AMONG THE TATTERS

(i)

Chalk a list of Erotic Commandments on your wall and enact their noble ends.

(ii)

Coat yourself with inertiaaah exuded from the day's dilapidated kernel.

(iii)

Pour inebriating Equivocals from tiny vials
to placate your acolytes with arcane tastes of abroad.

48.

TO CURE THE ANEMIC ANIMAL
LOOSE IN THE WEIRDERNESS

(i)

Eat roar vittles.

(ii)

Leave the territory of your frailty and pounce on the nearest of the whore-horned.

(iii)

Sink into your nourishing spoils and sleep off the Days of Ineffable Debris.

51.

TO AVOID BEING POISONED
BY THE DARKNESS IN THE RUCKUS CLUB

(i)

Twist your body into an inimitable torch and parade yourself on a haloed axis.

(ii)

Devour, Bleak Eater, devour the core of the snarl shroud.

(iii)

Your startling markings, spiked eyelashes, blinding hues:
enough to frighten any shadow-splattered brute-dresser.

53.

TO CAPTIVATE THE RECEPTIVE VESSEL
WITH SEDUCTION STABBINGS

(i)

Emit your little cult-calling pulsations
as far as the territorial fences of your illicit empire.

(ii)

Bend yourself into the overt shapes allotted to rapturous intrigue.

(iii)

The common language is that of the Inaudible Glint Verve.
Speak it with all your vernacular artistry embossed on the air.

54.

TO KEEP LUST ALIVE LONG AFTER
THE CONFLAGRATION HAS PASSED BY

(i)

Travel on untrod Scorch Paths, summoning up all the gall of your brazen nudeness.

(ii)

Recite once more the erogenous epics that you scrawled
down the length of your body in the Days of Epileptic Intimacy.

(iii)

Sleeplessly lie curled around your partner's embers.

63.

TO GO WHERE THE BLISS BABES ARE MATING

(i)

Hail, with a fearless composure, a reckless wagon to assail the turbulent thickets.

(ii)

Carry in you the sneer-blowers darts to tingle with reception from unformed skies.

(iii)

O Grand Plotter of the Carnal Charts, advance outside yourself
with the trajectories of your flares lighting the sprawling dimensions.

68.

TO PROTECT THE CREATIVE CORTEX
FROM A STULTIFYING INDECENCY

(i)

Surround yourself with the staves of precision,
intense ceremonies of accountability.

(ii)

Work on, in your solitary cell,
scribbling out little soul-shields made from fantastic sorceries.

(iii)

Bristling in your mock weaponry,
allow your carnal roars to quieten the wheedling devastations.

69.

TO ATTRACT THE SENSE-STARVED
OVER THE MAYHEM LINE

(i)

Stock an assortment of those spicy thrillpills that you can put
under your tongue and shiver with forbidden frenzies.

(ii)

You are a Song Duelist laying down your glove to unruly ears.

(iii)

O the attraction of the illegible.
Erect your corporeal emblem for all to wonder at.

70.

TO REMOVE THE LID FROM THE FESTIVE OPUS

(i)

How refreshing the clear absolutes are.
Close your dark dictatorial scriptures and look around
at the surrounding brightness.

(ii)

Rip off your garish rude robes and reveal the branded
heraldry of your erotic lexicon.

(iii)

Ply yourself from your burning diligence
and weather the confragations of the firing squad.

72.

TO TRACE DISTANT BLOOD-BEATING MESSAGE
TO THEIR ANATOMICAL KERNELS

(i)

Hark! Semaphoric sighs out of the Bleak.
Listen with your skin, prickly with dispatches from the illicit orbits.

(ii)

The torrential currents within a single voice.
Return to the source through the weirs and falls.

(iii)

Stain with your sentient dyes the cravings that leak from open arms.
Hunt down every hue.

81.

TO ASCEND ABOVE THE INTERNAL RUPTURE
AND STAND RESPLENDENTLY ANEW

(i)

Listen to your trusty full-throttled friend who washes you with
the purge-balm of the Enormous Experience.

(ii)

Take command on the heights overseeing the ol' Squirm Sea of your dominion.

(iii)

Sprinkle your body with the Breathing Spices to Perpetual Dazzlement.

88.

TO REACH THE SPAWNING POOLS
OVER THE BARBED ENIGMATIC MOUNTAINS

(i)

Strip away your clinging scaly and sodden carapace,
wash off your pungent rutting scents
and walk anew with a halo of bristling emptiness.

(ii)

Arrive on your sexual slay drawn by the bright energies of visionary orgies.

(iii)

Ascend the Weir of Immaculate Wreckage, your phantasmagoric fins cleaving
the downpour, the sacrificial juice of all bard-dom oiling your heroic voice.

from
THE ROAR ROOMS

SPLATTERHEAD

1

O Darling Veracity Dart, O Darling Veracity Dart, O Darling Veracity!
Dart!
You, O DarlingVeracity Dart, You, O Darling Veracity Dart, You,
Dart…
in m', in m', in m'……uhhh!

i'LL SHAVE M' SONG OF ALL EXPLICIT MELODY
'N' RECITE THE TRUE BARBS 'N' BONES

This is **not** the room f' Incipient Doses
(*used on y' fingertips across y' breast*)
but a
p(l)ain (c)old fashion'd intimacy
dissected int' (un) timely conquests…..

wi' the *softenin'* o' y' features in the *"Bardtimes"*
as i describe the………
………*Parallel Love Peregrinations*

'n' the explorations are positioned

'n' flame-trimmed   'n'   deadly accurate
as y' spurr'd determination
rides off

with y' leanin' back, headsingin':

"We drink the first Devilry Shots down in one!"

'n' the search is on f' a spot where the light disguises the ravages.

2

'ere *the Resilient Changers*

   are   chattin'

over their morning manna

in dome-wigs 'n' avocet eyebrows   'n' "i" over'ear

    The Distillate o' the Stretched Birthpangs
in snippets, :   ;   ,   .

collectin' 'em t' cure the withered wrist i 'ave.

I'LL 'AVE A SLICE O' THAT SQUIRMIN' VISTA IF Y' DON'T MIND.

  <u>This remarkable stroll</u>

speary   with the   embedded Vitals

i   replenish   m'   thirst by bearin'

        m' eyes.

  Look deep int' the Swill

 Arch Rabid '   :   'n'   *am startled!*

Put on the "Ahhhhhhhhhh" goggles, Rote One.

7

i 'ave learnt t' scream in the Blare Thicket with rhythmical eloquence

words of immense beauty...

WILL WHIP Y', LITTLE TORPID TOP.

They are lettin' smoke spout from their mouths, nodheads.

Serenity swarms on m',
implacable accord o' banishments,
death-winks,
neuter fingerin's

till y' worth (& y' identical kind) load these 'ands with youth-salts,
stabbin' scents 'n' the first indescribable actions

T' SAVE ME...

Carve a fresh song Leader of the Pelt in the mad rain. Drinkin' the pure amour-juice
we lie down 'n' relate 'ow sorcery 'as smashed the barriers 'n' I enter

& y' branded staff with the virgin motifs, y're stridin' against the flow & they wave
& shout: THERE'S KING SCALP! SHEAR ON!

Reading
THE SCAR COLLECTIONS
(bountiful pages of existence)

13

'N' i who wanted t' settle

m' 'ead on a holy comfort 'uh,

so much f' **MATURITY!**

i ALIGHT 'N' F L Y.

It's a pity
the darts *lose their* **in ten sity** *but* *in a*
new neck *are ....*
potently tipped f' the Oblivion Trail/Thump Path.

Announcin' the cold parameters (she

cropped 'er hair t' 'er skin
so 'er body grew in proportion)

Y' drug-tipped breasts!

Vast fallin'

comes
with t
he ascen
t
—BOY ABYSS fell int' 'imself

dragged 'is song 'eaddress around

collapsed at 'er feet 'n' slept 'n' woke new.

17

Callipered   ,

          m' Totem Figure.

The

                    remoteness

('as become familiar   )..............as i kiss y' knuckles.

The   Ripened walls ....clustered with y' *Fleshfruits*

          pl

                    un

                              g

                                        e

               d   o   w   n
'n' shower 'n' stain another s   p   l   a   y   ed day int' **life**.

18

As we are wrest together

i   am   privileged   t' be treated   t' y'   Long Flowin' Barb
Dance,

                  sway-waist

                  with the

                      dri p
                         p

                         i

                         n

                         '

                  j   o   y   s

that idles   through   gullies

                  with

     THE SEXHERD IN THEIR SEASON,   studded, antlered,
                        nuzzlin' the cheek.

20

Y' wear the Vulva Shoes & glide the Risk Room in an anthem cloud
& we stab it as it is & dive in our eyeclaps through the night. Yell on!

Yell on! Yell OM!

Spiritual treasure, body feats, the song spoils

as   i   ANNOUNCE   M'

Majestic Entrance

'n' pilin' out   in angular frantic burnin'

the   conjecture

                                                seeks   it's own

MERCY

in   wayward   introductions.

Fervour King, put on y' Screamin' Skull Crown

'n'

we're the ambassadors.

21

New shoots pushin'

through   the palms,

   y' earthly dress   fluted from the waist,

                    ,

rustlin' 'air as y' 'and passes through,   ,

        eyes   **dr**   e   **dg**   in   '

   the ol' dark miraculous wilderness.

You, tall gracious core, stand with m'—Beacon Babe,
        a reference t' the good root i've bin buryin'
              under the Slut Clinkers, the Sluice Sugars, the Clang Dancers

   'n'

        t   h   e   w   i   therin' is revived.

                                        Whew!

        Bring out y' Intensity Kit

'n' lay   'ands 'n' 'ands   over   'ands 'n' 'ands.

24

Y' tutelage is ingrained in m' side so i can stand in the blazin' century

<u>alone</u>
in painless tattoos that i will read later when i teach y' t' be illiterately sculptured,
a shriek-nuptial beckonin' the sensual chords already releasin' their
frazzled hormonics in a steamy mirage.

POUNCE on **MEEE!**

Deliver meee!

Walkin' out   in2   the   spired   ceilings

i

inhale bright fires

walkin' the   live   furrows quite   receptive.

There is no known antivenin
t' the nip & gore,
the flirt-tunes for the unwaxed,

the levitation o' principle,
crushed standards with scents
dropped ont' breasts,

the illicit bonds sprung,

go pulse & live through the unbearable equations

f' the rich nightly sauce will make the huntin' palatable,

Fierce Lipstickler!

27

You, Ms. **Jolt**, 'ave entered

with blunt tongues t' duel the sorceries o' Boy Abyss.

i will purge   the rot   from   m' body,

unfold   'n'   *nakedness*   protrudes

the inner branded drawin's   that direct m'   in2

the New Scales.

THE LOVESTACKS ARE BURNIN'!

By their light i see m' 'ands decorated with the Eternal Code o' y' Age 'n' want t'
maim myself further.

GLARE int' it......   & impale   the flesh shoots

glowin' through the new carpet.

'ere is y' new sustenance,   , Aortal Spike o' the Inroads,

clandestine conqueror,

the cups we drain.

28

Ward off the sexslings,
               they're 'urlin' projectories across the room.
In y' own barbed hoops y' want t'

        B a smokesman of love, m' fiery friend.

THESE UNTAMABLE TERMS ARE EXPECTED,

    "BURY 'IM IN THE WRITHE AVIARY," says the Muck Testament.

        The collection
             is   g e t t i n ' *vast,*
                 the Blindin' *DECIBELLS* toll
                      ,
        bleedin' vows   'n'   m'

Sleepless Encounters   awake   on a   whiff o' the
                              anodynes

in search   o'   the   most obvious *oblivion* ,

                             kind stimulants,
motherly jabs,   fondle-proof   *but*   with blatant features o' the
undernourished heart.

Unchristened in prophetic horns at the performance
                    we eventually swap dote-cards.

    Y' blemishes are y' beauty.

29

i PASS M' ENDANGERED THOUGHTS T' Y'...
                        NO SACRED UNION

                              lies
in y' enunciated chest   f' i   need the loyal dictum of y' kindred tongue

'n' not

the body-beggars starvin' menu.

                        It takes   l   o   n   g t' perfect
this edit 'n' rip out y'   lusty nails   t' replace   'em with
                    cool refreshing policies.

Makin' m' way
                up
                    the stairs
                        int' the *Blizzard Loft*
                                    i repeat
                                        the stun-phrases,

m' little bleedin' amulets shinin'
                            their potentials.

36

The unquietened Spoils Club,   **WRATH CHILD,**

the diggin' in the vigor vein.

Dare y' t' wear the Oblivion Uniform
                    with the flamin' nipples on the breast pockets

                frayed at the hips.

It is all etched, scoured on the plaque o' y'. Quite readable by damned codes,
seethin' initials, hyperglyphics, blood braille, common throngs.

Y've caught the *SONG PLAGUES.*

Do the *EMBER BOP* in the glimmerin' neighbourhoods.

Haunt the parlors o' the *OBSCENE TRACIN'.*

The wallowin' waiters are f' the settlin' o' *CLARITY TINCTURES,*

                y' 'airflame flickerin' from the roots.

CONFINE ME AS i GUST IN,

                thorny embraces

                'n' uncut in the quiet destinies that bludgeon

t' find the Ravages quite prim, kinda kissed in mute obedience in the lair.

41

O.K., i'll pick up the sting-elixir to start the evening,

we'll sit around Warpin'

& end... plunge-hilted, reap drawn, spine set with alarmin' gems!

NECTAR BULLET!

Unique shaped bruises

up

the

stairs

'n'

int' the impregnations

glowin' with initial sacred edges   but scuff off the coil

'n' down t' the bare fire-ribs.

IN THE SHADOWY COVEN the masterly irascible conversations

are quelled by touch,

the sexual flex.... down y' blazin' blouse.

43

The Rages are sleek, long-legged, runnin' nimbly across the wondrous interiors....
.....missin' crucial turns.......
.........but wrigglin' int' bed with the 1st minor flaw in the armor.

The RAVAGE BELL tinklin' on the lobes,

y' lawless beads,　　　　　m' truth punch　,　　　the burstin' Jangle Song,

'n' *THE HURLIN' O' SOULS AGAINST THE WALL, DOE BOY.*

i　　am　　SPIKED.... with delirium dust.... the fun warp.

O LONG LUST BROTHER... *are y' ready t' claim the crown?*
　　(*'n' whistle the smittened int' the pen?*)

There's a wild addled　　　　　fornication　　abroad
　　　　　　　as if　　　　　　the wind is rattlin' charmed lives.

　　We wait.... injected with diabolical understandin'
that there are unfurlin' arms around the corner...... perched abandon...'n'....
beautiful indecision..... rippin' **us** between the timorous wombwelds 'n' the
　　Great Growl ....tightenin' in the collar hold.

　　　　　　We waver in our howl-shroud
　　as　　y'

　　　　　　sidle　in

　　　　　　　　　with　intuition　　rearin'

& 　　knowin' meee

　　　　by the　precious fragment i wrap up f' y'.

44

Get out y'   corpus heat-urn   t' sway y' lush thinkin'.

      It's the key t' the SEX CELLAR
                               but i'm goin' off in m' own winged irreverencies,

                             buck-ups,
laconic lingo-harem strippin' f' mee.

        M' pedigree decor
                        o' the day's Plume o' Pangs... spangled rant,
our juggled ingredients in the miraculous throes, the tussle dives...

      o' OUR WOMB TRINKETS.

The 'aemorrhaging 'ere,   misconceptional votive scales
               linin' 'er smooth beatin' brackets,   the scent-drenches...
as once the ol' night-rot bursts out the scene in indelible stings.

      The tragic elopement o' the seconds, as we sit 'n' watch...

      <u>the bellicose beauties move fire.</u>

LIMP THE HERMETIC HURDLE, y' enlightenin' cures sproutin' inside,

      y' cell needle tinglin'   as   the New Diabolics   BLOOM
the (7th deadly) SINPHONY... orchestratin' the steps through the Brotherly Wail.

      Y' walkin' explosive joints are m' votive flame.

46

THE HOMAGE KLUB IS IN SESSION
('n' m' presidential fury-tuft is on).

Y' lingo is the slurred epidemic o' the Eclipsin'

'n'   they shovel in f' the blessin'

with their ferocious   ponytails   clinkin' 2 the creakin' dogma
    that the CHARISMATICS o' the Spiced Ear   litter,
2B   dabbed in   reverence
                                    on y' whole enlightenment

        BUT

            y've bin blastin y'self with yell radiation

'n' y' eyes are distempered in explosive tattoos.

WAIT, BABY, ... in the next room   y're goin' t' be revered

        ...f' y' cheek whittlings.

The listless Mouth Anthem soaks the air in 'ere,

    TORRENT, AH, TORRENT, STRIKE ALONG M' SHORE

'n'   i   muster m'   warrior germs f' new plagues,
    the barren floor
                    with not a... speckled breasted **thrash**   in sight.

49

Wear the brazen wig

'n'

bring intrepid interpretations...

int' the SMASH PIT...

...the rivet look, the Slink 'n'...

SIP Y' CATATONIC T' CHANGE THE COURSE O' 'ISTORY

as   the

art o' resuscitatin', the all-bland (100% fiberless)
is the participation o' the evening....

We'll meet... the **Turmoil Twins**,   ,   ,
livin' on void-crumbs,
shoppin' f' the new ephemerality,
SUDDENLY BLOTTIN' OUT!

Our motto: *The Rank Instinctive Brotherhood.*

55

WE'RE

...... the <u>unmuzzled nuclei</u>

devourin' the fast savagery within

t' deafen (BOOOOOM!) t' nullify

one unanimous route

across........... the hot mindstones...... f' another.

i EXTRACT EVERY NATURAL IMPULSE BY THE ROOTS

'n'

S.....P.....L.....A.....T.....T.....E.....R

m' inert ikons

with   HOLY LYMPH RAIN.

i am ajar....... whim cushion.

56

FLAME WELL, BOY ABYSS,

fructification   stuck   t' y'

RAUCOUS LIMPET,

dictatin' the experience-spit

as

it is   sp   l   a   tt   ed   all   over   the   place.

An innocuous saunterin'   in 'n' out   the   *BELCH EMPORIUMS*

bre.....akin'

int' the Peeled Onslaught .

ANOINTED WITH ACHES

the

OBLIVION BROTHERS 'AVE FOUND A CAREER

o' lucid blackouts, coded infinities

'n' jacktrap from mouths

issuin' the fabulous oaths

o' clustered fraternities,

yap inoculations.

58

'N'   i

          remain glazed   above the   FLESHSWELL.

     The mocean,   the fecundity cove   pourin'

its...........veins............with............squeal.............elixirs,

          hormonal snuff,,,,,,,,

               pulse peelers,,,,,,,

                    'n' the cascade aortics,,,,,,,.

TO BE A RECEPTOR....... dart-hog,   a clamour seer,   torrid-tipped

          halo

                                        sailin'

          with immunity's laugh

                    down the aisles.

SPLATTERHEAD

from
THE THRONGSONGS
A Book of Chants

The chants provide a twice daily reading over the duration of a year.
They are on the offensive only in that they are incentives,
in that they are auspicious spurs to beseige life with.
They signal an attack "with a soul gaff; in epic wrath-rituals;
as a caracature of the *Blizzard Ikon*; by the *Cult of Nill*;
when your Jolt Collar is on the last notch."

(A selection of a.m & p.m. readings)

ONE

a.m.

1. Attack by the attentive nurturing of an inchoate passion.
2. Attack till an incandescence runs in to drown the dark ignobility.
3. Attack the terrain stung with the carrion echo of the Sublime Invocation.
4. Attack to the hilt, charging through your dens in laugh spurs.
5. Attack the homily proclaiming "The Savage Scapegirl Cometh."
6. Attack in a supra-moral din outfit, blanking out with it on.
7. Attack as your addictive cadence infects the maelstrom.
8. Attack at once archaic and as a newly born herald.
9. Attack when skinned of your drum pelt, Absorbent Oracle.
10. Attack by singing "O Infatuation! O Babe Assassin! Is that you?"
11. Attack when capped in totemic quiffs.
12. Attack those christened the Disturbed Abyss Supremacists and calm them.
13. Attack as a precursor to holocaustic swoons.
14. Attack the single protracted desire splicing the sexes.
15. Attack the immortal umpire, his circulatory ooze, his helix finger.

16. Attack using the Diabolical Scriveners to fabricate your life.

17. Attack when rubbed with contagious grace in the Snare Club.

18. Attack the Supreme Object.

19. Attack by ceremonious mask-splitting to redeem the inert imago.

20. Attack in a fertile vehicle.

21. Attack with your thaumaturgic fingers dipped in protective elixirs.

22. Attack in the caricature of the mythical Blizzard Icon.

23. Attack the origin of your moral formulae set in a corolla of ataxia.

24. Attack when outfitted in the pomposity of a blazing junta.

25. Attack in enlightened epidemics.

26. Attack with a religiosity melded from the Two Thighs of Enactment.

27. Attack punctually at the strike of the Ravage Bell.

28. Attack the flagrantly absurd residue that authority has on its tongue-tracks.

29. Attack by growing the most devastating proportions from the human seed.

30. Attack as an educator, teaching the erotic brands of your caste.

31. Attack by a lyricism deployed for its stark reflective absolutism.

FOUR

p.m.

1. Attack to possess your prey's intimacies.
2. Attack while you plait your fully nourished shapes into grandiloquent temporal announcements.
3. Attack by maturing into a hedonistic totem.
4. Attack with the strands of your vibrancy lashing the length of your culture.
5. Attack as an impaler, an amulet, the only trembling indicator.
6. Attack to repatriate the suckling Kid Wallop.
7. Attack with your plumage soaked in vials of Great Thump Scent.
8. Attack with your purified prints sizzling across the rude dunes.
9. Attack by heat etiolation, Little Blister Bundle.
10. Attack as the only insidious weapon left sparpened.
11. Attack the ol' turbidity, fertilized to the tip.
12. Attack in the Decibel Dens by wringing out the lust factors from them.
13. Attack nocturnally, fusing First Human Longing with its twin.
14. Attack the tongue-drum that lies sleeping within the chaotic poles.
15. Attack as an effulgence rises over you.

16. Attack over the havoc lines, covertly singing into the Quick Blazes.

17. Attack the Jargoness, annoying with her ultimate anvil.

18. Attack when you have couched your skin in grand hued ridicule.

19. Attack as a discriminate Smotherer.

20. Attack in your bewildering writhe tunic.

21. Attack the notorious shards that injure the orbits of purity.

22. Attack the darkened cove with hallowed syllables moving freely in their beds.

23. Attack with your adoration for the molded lovely form.

24. Attack by lancing the canopies, by fighting to burst your encirclement.

25. Attack as an engulfed cornucopian character, an exiled apostate.

26. Attack when the imbalance topples the Mortal Seizures over into the Inhaling Swell.

27. Attack till the Plunges carry the tingling litter into the wallow pools.

28. Attack the honey hips welded into a sublime spire.

29. Attack the underlined passage in the Great Book: Woe Be to Thou.

30. Attack by raising swoon-blisters over the field of insatiability.

FIVE

a.m.

1. Attack to eternally mutate the character reference written in soul sap.
2. Attack when rabid and dumb-strung from a line hung in
      the Boil 'Em Sanctum.
3. Attack as you alight and devastate those in their awe.
4. Attack the funneled Intoxicants who contrive new deities up ahead of you.
5. Attack as one of the sonorous calls flowing over the Crackerat Runs.
6. Attack when the Bright Notion lashes you with its remissive standard.
7. Attack the circuitry that facilitates the blissful blackouts you transcend to.
8. Attack by spangled drug-boxing and flips into the voidom.
9. Attack under the glare and domination emphatic in a sharp eye.
10. Attack as the tantrum colors give life to the plain rhythmical congress.
11. Attack all the exposed virtues through the seams that will not be clamped.
12. Attack as an epiphenomenon, plonking around in your miraculous plague-wear.
13. Attack the clenched bud and have it splay 'n' split 'n' taste the forlorn.
14. Attack to extol your Gnash Law.
15. Attack in the bleak doorways, your pungency the interminable amulet.

16. Attack when knowing what the Word weighs.

17. Attack what blank necessity denotes the Deal of your Day.

18. Attack by growing taller than your parental corolla.

19. Attack as a courageous satellite, your determined stride
    emphasizing your radiance.

20. Attack the bastard pose stuck monolithically through the earth.

21. Attack with your cadence speaking above and below the Bland Line.

22. Attack the silt plastered in the delinquent eddies.

23. Attack as a forum for the wail-hunter, the spitter.

24. Attack with distinction, stupendous pips awarded for scuffling in the Froth.

25. Attack from the kiln you have thrown youself into.

26. Attack by interpreting the cacophonies issuing from the Wrought Instrument.

27. Attack by remembrances that block the flight into your precious atrium.

28. Attack those balking at the cupped light you handle.

29. Attack till the social rind is cajoled.

30. Attack in a reversal of the rarefied plunder-gospel set aloof and inert.

31. Attack with libations anointing the grizzled homes, residencies smelling
    of wrecked honors.

EIGHT

p.m.

1. Attack in mutable uni-logues arching over the wires into the New Bareness.
2. Attack when the harbor floods with the Lovable Pang Harvest.
3. Attack by dangling arcane beast-ornaments from your projections.
4. Attack in a huge vehicle piled with the Contagion Kin.
5. Attack the guile-walkers, spice decoys deflecting the true furrow.
6. Attack after the ecstatic aria bursts within the cap.
7. Attack with the indivisible guises fast on your corporeal sculpture.
8. Attack while a neuro-cotyledonous storage is pithed with lengthy Flirt Needles .
9. Attack by rudely plying the shoulders apart to reach the sequestered gem.
10. Attack an anemic nudity beneath the Bleating Shroud.
11. Attack the certitude of the ashen-sided martyr's unshakable deliberation.
12. Attack in your dance-mitre, seer-helmet, your shard-calls received.
13. Attack when recognized as the direct line to the Lyrical Spindle.
14. Attack to turn the bloodwheel through infernal interstices.
15. Attack with the last nourishment of manna you devour in the lamp's length.

16. Attack by mercies dug from under the heretical shield.

17. Attack by exorcising the ether with the cool ointments of veracity.

18. Attack to scale the net barbed with tactile intoxicants.

19. Attack to forge a marriage between the tyrannical Congealer and the Flickering Waif.

20. Attack to cleave your own igneous strata.

21. Attack in gratitude for the unfurled yells on the shore.

22. Attack with the breasts of a born Emblazer.

23. Attack with your Oblivion Syringe.

24. Attack to emulate the mesmeric conflagrations splintering into your tenderness.

25. Attack the inability to squeeze your somatic flushes through the Age Eye.

26. Attack as a pair of lit and brandished holy horns executing their little wrath.

27. Attack in an allusive song-visor.

28. Attack when honorably bade to lay with the fat pupate ones.

29. Attack with an elementary uproar.

30. Attack with poesy, sonorous fragments left to explain your entirety.

31. Attack by riding homeward-bound over the quake-swells.

NINE

a.m.

1. Attack the main manacle and free the Asphyxiated.
2. Attack your little ephemeral partner with the distillate of the minute.
3. Attack by flinging the salted aphrodisiacs and eye-dyes over the Hermaphrobites.
4. Attack in the Renewed Jolt, resuscitating the hands to crave again.
5. Attack when the tethers yank in the cells.
6. Attack the Bloodrunning in the Seam Aisles, the mini-rills of the Mange.
7. Attack as the Indelible One.
8. Attack till the Crushing Event absorbs itself in a pile of wild rendering.
9. Attack with a honed argon more powerful than any Blamhand.
10. Attack the sex decoys placed either side of the trap.
11. Attack the flawless surface of the irresistible Debacle.
12. Attack to be alive in the Inflammable Cores of each day.
13. Attack as a Spangled Elder possessing the first illegitimate word by appointment.
14. Attack with a diva's smothering command over her bare devotees.
15. Attack by kneading the blind hoot-ardors into the jaw.

16. Attack in the steps of the Violating Swath and the drunk Penetration Pioneer.

17. Attack in a writhe-ripple across the body to the ecstatic hilt.

18. Attack by scuffing off your yoke and flaming pillory.

19. Attack with no weapon save your most poignant slut-gun.

20. Attack when the reading of the Breed Annuals is intense.

21. Attack to give tactile faith its due for saving the demonic gush till last.

22. Attack between the inceptive tide marks upon your bare rostrum of wails.

23. Attack a generation's pabulum with graceful distortion.

24. Attack while the druglocks encase your dearest possessions.

25. Attack by coupling and cascading into one another at long last.

26. Attack by injecting a vectorial stream into the populace.

27. Attack to rekindle the visceral pyro-rippers in your own abyss.

28. Attack the venomous provocateurs down the long Sting Furrows.

29. Attack while still yearning for the great life-flaring storylines.

30. Attack in remembrance of the Blade Brother's trek into the Barrens.

TEN

a.m.

1. Attack with your visceral prongs lowered

2. Attack in your cloven hair, infamously a fountain to behold.

3. Attack as a Serpentine Peeler, as the Goddess to Eruptive Splendor.

4. Attack by reading the Thrash Testaments aloud.

5. Attack repeatedly the inexperience until the core pours with Whole Nourishment.

6. Attack in an interpretation carved from the lean erotic stunts you frame.

7. Attack to pick your revelation off the littered aisle in the Beaten Humdrums.

8. Attack by a reflex-lexicon, by communiques of eyeless dance cant.

9. Attack, you Ambidexter, you with pole-spines spinning, you torrential Glare.

10. Attack to insert your mold under the animated effigies prowling the slime-boards.

11. Attack when variegated and dyed with foreign tinctures.

12. Attack by going to inquisitorial lengths to find sensual equivalents for immediacy.

13. Attack along the intra-skull nuptial trail imprinted with clean scare-marks.

14. Attack after the unleashing you deemed to be a climax loses its sanctuary.

15. Attack as a custodian of the Great Vatic Heap.

16. Attack in a cockeyed halo hat.

17. Attack while supine and exhausted in the heydays of the force fields.

18. Attack with your edicts of grace meted out on the scream-studded denizens.

19. Attack the itinerant soul scraps entering the jibe-hive's consecrations.

20. Attack when empirical demands lurch out and sting immunity's rascals.

21. Attack to transfer the Blare Lore from your perfect muteness.

22. Attack by bargaining with a pagan currency, the exchange of
    the illicit plague stubs.

23. Attack on the prodigal spot, scorched, revered as a kissing pulpit.

24. Attack to save the superlative clause for the hermetic orgy.

25. Attack by branding the illegible character 'Tethered' on your fertile loam.

26. Attack even when the sigh ploughs a long trench through the dark nest.

27. Attack in a hubbub wardrobe, your pleats bleeding the absolute corpus.

28. Attack as a hybrid shadow in the level expanses of the vulnerable.

29. Attack the craft of employing the eye-masks for the benefit of the trust-tilled.

30. Attack with the immortal patience of a Bile Sniper.

31. Attack after your prodigies have left the Barb's enclosure for good.

ELEVEN

a.m.

1. Attack with a soul gaff.
2. Attack as you preen your heroic cockscomb.
3. Attack from adventurous angles the choral epicenter of your song.
4. Attack on the stairs leading to the horizon illuminated by
   your natural radiation.
5. Attack once again, in the familiar trench, the fierce metabolism.
6. Attack when knotted in your Paradigm Cap and your Flirt Blinkers.
7. Attack without a hint of snarl-cream on your cheeks.
8. Attack on the short march between the Verbal Throes and
   the Embedded Prose.
9. Attack with your squalor-collar lit with enriched sex plumes.
10. Attack by rallying to the heraldic torsos scrawled with desperate creeds.
11. Attack the clamped bastion to make it pour forth the communiques.
12. Attack when the enfeebled tenets ordain the habitual surges.
13. Attack in the knowledge that your chasm-twinges are tidal.
14. Attack by raking over the spawning fields you have laid in.
15. Attack with nubile fingers searching the rough troughs.

16. Attack to relinquish the unwedded authority from the New Roar Regime.

17. Attack in memory of the passage from one eternal journey to another.

18. Attack by downing the shreik-pail in one slug.

19. Attack as you analyze your own parched drive into the Nub of Idolatry.

20. Attack the light dens you frequent with your dark glares.

21. Attack when the impassioned propositions are peeling from the dud mouths.

22. Attack through the Slum Groves in search of unleashed cures.

23. Attack without the pain associated with the 3rd Degree of Grappling.

24. Attack by perverting the thin songs before their prime.

25. Attack till you fructify.

26. Attack the frail shells encasing the Chronicles of an Abrasive Life.

27. Attack the upheavals wreathing your head.

28. Attack the pursed oracle so as to let it blurt out the Great True Whine.

29. Attack on null-tinctures that are fanning through your fleshthrone.

30. Attack in your thorny ear-caps, your shatter-plumes, your sacred sigh-gear.

TWELVE

p.m.

1. Attack by being the shining fixture in the Scrawl Crib.
2. Attack as an incarnate code.
3. Attack the home turfs, the remnants of your word-womb, your mother.
4. Attack the birthbarks, epidermal growls, hypothalamic-howls.
5. Attack after teasing the holy bud from the Gnarl at Large.
6. Attack by drinking deeply from the long fire jugs offered to the Blessed.
7. Attack the inviolable vocal mortar secreted in your personal carnal drum-slum.
8. Attack the model abyss with its exclusive membership to the New Addled Age.
9. Attack on sensual stilts.
10. Attack when the umbilical guidelines are ignored.
11. Attack in a troupe entertaining the Decadent Monopoly with a priceless rumpus.
12. Attack those who wear the spiky girdles, the molded topography.
13. Attack in your bliss-lashes and your bruising glares–the apparel of the Age.
14. Attack as a chain-stroker of glossy pelts.
15. Attack the aspiring Ms Rivet at the springhead.

16. Attack under the I-clamps, with your quiff-bonnet sprouting
     above the Breathers.
17. Attack in cult-diva armor, hedonistically prickling in your vulgar tantrums.
18. Attack by standing in a position to receive a demigodly unction.
19. Attack when the inebriating whine becomes too much for your singing sap.
20. Attack with toots of imbecility while snouting through Insipia.
21. Attack the One who brings a change of hallucinogenocidal clothes.
22. Attack with crafted sieges waged under the United Entanglement Emblem.
23. Attack as the Bleeding Bragpipe calls your loyal Drugoons to you.
24. Attack by heeding none of the Singing Sage's leviathan obstacles.
25. Attack after the discreet uppercut to your soular-plexus.
26. Attack with a renewed spew of the ol' larval missiles from the Human Spring.
27. Attack as the brotherhoods are worn once again with cocked complicities.
28. Attack the nature of your obverse profile that penetrates the inner odyssey.
29. Attack after hurling your Immaculate Diagrams over those without resistance.
30. Attack by changing headgear as you roar inside your besieged clarity.
31. Attack with your Jolt Collar on the last notch.

SPLATTER

from
INK MUSIC

HEAD

WHERE THE YOUTHETTES
DIE OF IMMORTALITY

Dark on the pale flesh
The hunter and the prey undress
Stand the little innocents all at play
A single knot of flame within their braids

And the time will come
To the heart's dark slum
When she of the thin-wearing thighs will speak
In a dark-splashing lingo-larynx that bleats
Out a song: The Inferno Nest of the Yelp-Skinned Lost Youthette
BANG! Hear the gong-songs rattle
In the throat, in the arms, "we all fall down"
Come the Brute Throats: MARCH LOAD MARCH through Jolthead Town
To scatter the streets of the vivid red-mouthed Flesh Skinners
Furiously drunk on synapse sap and ol' oblivion thinner
O clear the streets, babe. Hail to the slum-drum

And the pale-combed boygirl sips life

In the bar the masketeers
Pass the six hundred and sixty-six sins of the beautiful girlboy
While on the screen, the jerk-back of heads
The smooth-toned duos and the mow-haired ripple-backs dance
Jugged up on small delights given freely
To wrap their little souls in a numb-snuff sorcery trance
and it's "You there, ENTERTAIN ME!"
(With your body swaying on owl-egged calves)
Where "THERE'S NO PLACE LIKE HOME"
Spills spilling out from the Syrup King's heart

And in Reflex Rooms of sheer red and raw-spangled kingfisher
Hoot Heads cocked sideways like bright-throated birds
Barearmed music from the eardrummers comes
As giggleful kidlings giddy on "slop"

Speak jagged dancing of rapidity
And the youthettes die of immortality
Clothed in cinnabar and raptured ochre.

Their masks, terrified and restless, fain gentility
(*O these sneaky Tranquillians*)
While the only color is of the brilliant red hearts
That burns on their breasts
And the slim kindle of flame in their hands

O see how the Shimmer King's body is burning
And she in garnished ardor is wearing
The tempest of the slum-drums final fling
And the bells of hunger and the bite they bring

FROM INVISIBLE FIRE FOR THE INNOCENT

Invisible fire for the innocent
Juggling sand for the wide-eyed
Miracles under the belt
The triple-jointed wrists of stealth

Pulling smoke-screens from the sleeve
Dry water in jars, secret potions in shoes
Healing the well, blinding the bright
Sawing the soul in two

Slight-of-hand rearrangements of air
Skeleton keys for bodies laid bare
The Delusive Disciple Drug staining the lips
Their stupid glares in my grip

Afflicted masks for the beautiful at heart
Stoops for a stance of youth

In the Sanctum of Sorcery the veil will reveal
The old are born, the well-to-do are heeled

*   *   *   *   *

I reel with ancestral ecstasies in these writhe-high aisles
"For thine is the fever"
Arch-angelic Iridescents, mystics of the Last Morass and the Junk Jackals
    of the Blasted
"For thine is the fever"
The Buoyant Braves in splayed skin-wings, genetic extension gadgetry
"For thine is the fever"
Rumble-muzzles and flickering sense-siphons
"For thine is the fever"
Girls displaying thighs of slippery silver, swigging Ataxia Tonics,
    loading swoon-rifles
"For thine is the fever"
Niavanaaahs, cranked-up karma in the Orphan Age
"For thine is the fever"

Scream grafts and braille songs of Father Phantom and the Tendril Tongues
"For thine is the fever"
Quiver Things rattling through the Debacle Zone casting oracles of briquette bone
"For thine is the fever"
Miming the Raw Whore, the Fleshy Fruit
"For thine is the fever"
Disembodied Buddies under the Imbecilic Roof

Ah, The Eruption Rites! The Eruption Rites!
I am ready to receive 'em
Ah, The Eruption Rites! The Eruption Rites!
Bring on the blessed fever

I walk through the Street of Sexterranians, aquanauts space out on magma milk
"For thine is the fever"
Head Kegs imploding in the Hemorrhage House
"For thine is the fever"
Stalagmighty minaret wigs on the High Detectors, Intravenous Swamp Salvations
"For thine is the fever"
Incarnation faucets pouring, express hibernation fits
"For thine is the fever"
The epidemic mire-dancers and the women in their third-eye robes
"For thine is the fever"
At the Amnesia Oasis, on high-hoof shoes, the Bombers are
      gargling rotation liquor
"For thine is the fever"
The Psycho-Lasso Lads shoot virile venom, speak the elastic classic,
      ol' Overdose Bicker
"For thine is the fever"
Stingleaders and Young Fertilizers in mating barbs
"For thine is the fever"
Vertebrae seizures and blotto-visions at the Planetary Plague Fiesta
"For thine is the fever"
The Myth-Pimp of Miracles and the Ripened Readies, Squirmers and
      the Urban Burners
"For thine is the fever"
The Convulsion Kid with elevator eyes (on other floors)
"For thine is the fever"
Fiery Lifetime Vendors bootlegging coma-aroma
"For thine is the fever"
The Kosmic Rodeo Kult is riding again on the backs of Alto-Orgasm Creatures
"For thine is the fever"
Bodies branded with illuminant glyphs and tattoos of the Resurgent Serpent
"For thine is the fever"

Ah, The Eruption Rites! The Eruption Rites!
I am ready to receive 'em
Ah, The Eruption Rites! The Eruption Rites!
Bring on the blessed fever

       *   *   *   *   *

I have resigned from bland histrionics
Newness, renown, and reputations
I have become blind to the sound of my own language
Preferring the pomp and glory of revelations

For I can fly like Sister Kingfisher
Dazzling bright fury into darting blue
I can sing like Brother Kingpin
Throat deep, fever-pitched, and beautifully too
Wading on, through the Great Cranium Curfew
With the Goddess of Parasitic Bombardment Bliss
And the ambrosial urgency of her willow hips

"For thine is the fever"

       *   *   *   *   *

I am comatose
In beauty
Lulled, rocked
On bare shoulders
In my own world

I am perfectly blind
The solitary dreamer
Without regret or retreat

Breathing the pungency
Of my own miracle

"For thine is the fever"

THE BIRDHEAD BOYS

Wingbeat / beat / beat / beat...

The birdhead boy feels it in his heart
As he pushes back the feathers from his mask
And as he craves his girl against his wings
He opens her heart to taste the sweetness within
He feeds the fire in the flesh
Sips the squawk of the song
Licks the dark scent of rhythm from her arms
Living life on the limb dressed in all his wild wings

Wingbeat / beat / beat / beat...

O the birdhead boys
Flip flap in the trees
Dance like vaseline
Speak in striptease
With mascara mouths
And sugarplum eyes
They do the smoocharoo
Rude and new
Combing back
Their black-jack hairdos

And the birdhead girls
Spring up on their perches
To preen their throats
And soft nectared necks
They twitter and talk,
Do the Wagtail Walk
Burying their heads
Within their breasts

And wiping their feather-red mouths
On lover's lips
The rhythm slips
Out of their hips
They spill laughing from windows
Swoon-dipped larks
To cartwheel
Jumble-jerk and dance

And in the dim or dark
The curling of bodies goes on
While the throats of the Wild Wings
Peel out their songs

And in deep corners they cuddle up
Or fain frenzies cheek to cheek
The light-headed girls with the brilliant beaks
But still, the birdhead boys are drunk as diamonds
Bright as knives, balancing like ballerinas
Lifting up their long-legged necks
Shouting in their ticky-tacky tongues
Holding thin cigarettes between feathers and thumbs
Not much for talk but pigeon-toed slang and squawks

And the swan-necked girls sing:

Sugar up and knuckle down
We'll give you honey from our mouths
Dip your hands into our hearts
Lick the dark scent of rhythm from our arms

SWALLOWTAIL VIOLINS

And with the braids of beauty thrown back
Rare designs of slut dances against the hip
In the room that lets in furious light
Stand little statuettes with barbed red lips
Whose hearts still bare the sting
And scented on their pale skin
Posed in their cheekbones and wings
They drag their dances by the hair
And sweetly scalp the sound

Whip the dark rhythm on
Spur on the jagged song
Flex Muscle Music
On geometric saxophones
And dance the Naked Truth
In skin-shaped clothes

Do the crow-neck reflex
The nightjar strip
Sip thin white rhythm
In the dark
Jerk back the head
Again and again
Let swallowtail violins
Pierce the heart

And for those who wear
The slow red mouths
There's eternity
In the Moment House
Where painted limbs
In a barbiturate dance
Let swallowtail violins
Pierce the heart

And Radio Featherthigh
Squawks out loud
To splash the walls
With a shrapnel blast
O I'm your junkman
Your sweet-eyed snipe
Let swallowtail violins pierce the heart

MUSCLE AND HEAT

Sky and rhythm, drug and drum
Muscle and heart will never sleep
Feet and feather rise and leap
Muscle and heart will never sleep
Skin will splinter, day to dust
But muscle and heat will never sleep

Dancers darkening the world at its width
The sway of the heart on the hinge of a hip
Vein lanes rumbling with phantom fits
Such are the end of ecstasy in this

Quick-eyed and headless in the trees
Such are the ends of ecstasy
Quick-eyed and headless through shaken seas
Such are the ends of ecstasy
Feet and feather will rise and leap
Muscle and heat will never sleep
Quick-eyed and headless is the disease
On to the ends of ecstasy

SPLATTER

from
LIVING ON ROAR STREET
WITH THE WORLD AND HIS WIFE

HEAD

LIVING ON ROAR STREET WITH THE WORLD AND HIS WIFE

On Roar Street the World and his Wife walk with me, where the Great Stun of Life comes up and kisses me, giving me the most ecstatic of wounds, where I am covered from head to heel in a rain of the Throngsongs, where the thigh-hanging lingo enters my ears, where Little Tangle and Saint Riot are my friends, where we feast on the Very Moment and where I am carried shoulder-high through Frenzy Park and I hear them say: "Sweet dreams, Babe Inferno," pressing their lips on me, laying their arms over me, throwing me into the Burning Bliss Club, where there are new dances to dance and new songs to sing: *The Big Drain, The Sex Stuff, The Apocalypso, The Life,* where the Tongue of Noise is on our heads and we are cleansed and we move together and are knotted and loved and loved not, where there is a pleasure called Mercy, where there is a joy called Nothing, and all the eyes in here are full of it, but I, with my kingdrum whipping, bang on through this dreadful adoring darkness to stand out in Roar Street with the thrill-darts piercing, with my Howl Hat on, my Sensual Suit tailored.

This is where I live: on Roar Street with the World and his Wife.

I am deafened. I am overwhelmed. Burst over me.

Here King Drum comes.

SHAKE THE WHOLE WORLD
TO ITS FOUNDATIONS

You have nothing to fear
Perfection is coming
The sky is growing lighter
Perfection is coming
A strong dance needs a strong rhythm
Perfection is coming
Shake the whole world to its foundations
Perfection is coming

Attack with a new beauty
Attack with an immense invisibility
Attack with the streaming colours of your flags held aloft
Attack on silent feet
Attack at all times of the day
Attack with deliberate grace
Attack to kill the dark spirits
Attack with a million drums bursting
Attack with all the touch of your fingertips
Attack as a matter of life and death
Attack with the sweet scents pressed on you
Attack in seconds
Attack in an eternal fever
Attack by setting fire to the roof
Attack by being a child's hand
Attack by patience
Attack with the full intensity of your innocence
Attack with your charms written across your skin
Attack in ways not expected of yourself
Attack as a natural desire
Attack as a craftsman
Attack in the name of nothing and everything
Attack with burning sensations in both arms
Attack by placing yourself in a position of ecstasy
Attack the big belly of the storm

Attack with passion
Attack the bright red hurt
Attack with complete disregard for being mortal
Attack when the heart says "Now!"
Attack when the river lies with the sea
Attack when you must
Attack across the wide openings and into the unknown

Regather your forces as you rock to sleep the chaos doll in your arms
Regather your forces as you make a sign to protect your way through the darkness
Regather your forces as you slip on the beautiful patterns of your new skin
Regather your forces as you penetrate the rock with the songs of your deliberation
Regather your forces as you rattle the top branches of the tree until succulence falls

You have nothing to fear
Perfection is coming

Attack in the fertile period when the banks overflow
Attack with an auspicious symbol daubed down your chest
Attack using miracles
Attack when the prophecies are clearly wrong
Attack with a wealth of unleashed ambitions tucked beneath your arm
Attack by hypnotic movements
Attack as a huge bird swooping across the land
Attack in a headdress of bristling endeavours
Attack when the winds blow with and against you
Attack to the furthest point imaginable

This is no ordinary rain that refreshes your skin in these parched fields
This is no ordinary wind that cools you in this breathless valley
This is no ordinary fever that revives you in this languid sea
This is no ordinary voice that speaks to you in this silent cataclysm

Let all these echoes sound through your bones
No one bears fruit better than yourself
The sap is sweet

You have nothing to fear
Perfection is coming

Attack with the roaring instruments of your choral upheaval
Attack while reciting the human catechism that runs through your veins
Attack at the precise hour
Attack with magic
Attack with the clandestine propaganda of all great lovers
Attack before and after sinking into oblivion
Attack between lives
Attack by sprinkling cures from the witch doctor's rattle
Attack when you are destroyed outwardly but not inwardly
Attack with hair plaited in the ropes of your escape
Attack with a huge brush soaked in the most indelible ink

You have nothing to fear
Perfection is coming
The sky is growing lighter
Perfection is coming
A strong dance needs a strong rhythm
Perfection is coming
Shake the whole world to its foundation
Perfection is coming

ATOM BOY AND I ARE O.K.

Atom Boy and I are O.K.
With our jet-legs to get us out of here
With our bomb-fists to break us free
With our spike-heads to cleave
Clean through the skies
O Atom Boy and I won't die

We're the only real rockets around here
The only ones who know how to steer
Astronomical Arrows in our finest hour
Little sputnickles of phantasmagoric power

Atom Boy and I are O.K.
So say the Blam Babes / So say the Blam Babes
We're zoom bloomers on slick fin wings
Optimum drumboys of the new noise stings
Beautiful streams of smoke
Cruising the far reaches of eternity's coast.........

Hey, Atom Boy and I are O.K.
So say the Blam Babes / So say the Blam Babes
Hey, Atom Boy and I are O.K.
So say the Blam Babes / So say the Blam Babes
Hey, Atom Boy and I are O.K.
The fastest forms of life on the Great Gush Way
Hey................O.K.

O Atom Boy and I are O.K.
With our jet-legs to get us out of here
......out of here......out of here.....out o.......

ALL MY MUTINOUS MOLECULES

All my mutinous molecules bursting the skin
With weird freedom from the rush of the Eternal Eruption Rum within

O here I come singing that ol' grog song:

Peg-legged liver, gut tattoos
Venom-dipped pigtail and eel-skin shoes
I'm Yellow Dog, Atomic Bomb Beard
And on Spineless Street, I'm the one to fear

I ride behind a figurehead of long-horned words
In my low-slung spiritual guns and mesmerist's spurs
I have come to ravage the Reflexists, to broadside the Routeenagers
To pillage the smug zones, spring the cranium cages

Follow me through the short-skirted sea, the flotsam flesh
Under the Three Phallic Flames with smoke-plumed breath
With Psycho-slaves, Limboys, the Stuns, the Great Globs
I plunder, I ransack, I kidnap, I rob

O here I come singing that ol' grog song:

Peg-legged liver, gut tattoos
Venom-dipped pigtail and eel-skin shoes
I'm Yellow Dog, Atomic Bomb Beard
And on Spineless Street, I'm the one to fear

FROM THE GUIDE TO EVERYTHING ABSOLUTE AND FLEETING

The living and dying take place elsewhere

(I have been harassed by the notion of oblivion)
Leaving home in the gift of sacred wandering, nothing now seems the same . . .

Naturally, I could have told you how love was supposed to meet us
I, like you, have read *The Sublime Reaches*

We all remember the last page
"AND KNOWING I WILL ALWAYS BE WITH YOU,
I SIT UP LATE INTO MY LIFE."

What a book! Unforgettable! Even when the book is closed
We exchange these words for mortal practice

Cantering out in our plumed halters
To dazzle the days ahead

from

LAA...
The Dangerous Opera Begins

FROM LAA...

For Yoshimasu Gozo

ACT I

Laa... Immaculata!

Voyages! Dark pastures on this isle
I get up from my life, sing, laa...

The music sounds irrelevant when I dance.

I am backstage/damson/peridot/garnet/...tiaras...
      ...practicing blood cries...laa!

No chorus can compete with me!
   FLAME! FLAME! FLAME!

GOD...

   i...

   have to find my own voice...

  as I enter this city

laa... laa... laa...

     The dangerous opera begins

We come walking on like huge sails.

HAIL!

The Conch's call:

      "I am dead with life, Ms. Monsoon
      Take me, oar after oar, into your city"

From up here where I write (singing) laa...
"I see hysteria, baby / seething head over head over m' friends
      ah, a beautiful girl walking upright in her
         BURNING!

I want to say:

      "I WHO WAS ONCE A GOLDEN WOMAN
      WHO WALKED IN THE DARK HEAVENS
      BUT AM NOW GROWN OLD...ah,_____ laa!"

Matadors of Fire! I, wingbone jacket
      ... the chorus are braiding their hair, tying it back with wire so barbed...
(I want to be the audience but my heart is preaching such hell,
      I can only glide up and close my eyes...)

BRING ME THUNDER IN YOUR MOUTH!

 Behind the backdrop they are beating roofs of metal and crying with emotion:

"HER UNFORGETABLE BEAUTY! HER UNFORGETABLE BEAUTY!"

        The dangerous opera begins

laa _____,
laa _____,
laa _____, , , , ,

    "another bar, another blood sister"

I wish I could walk silently not disturbing
            the arrangement of my colossal character,

walking mutely through the holy fields......................

    My mouth is the Great Betrayer

 ,,, And being in command of this language I tell it to m...urder

       laa... (yes, in these days, you name it)

228

Voyages! Dark pastures on this isle
I get up from my life, sing, laa. . .

Walk with me a little, hold my hand
(something my dear, above all, quite natural
            and in your words "realistic")
Until in a hail of arms I am off again
            (an old woman's frail soul)
STRIDE OFF! HAIL! STRIDE OFF!

Dressed in my worldly mockery
I refuse to face the facts
Lined up throughout life
Like dead fish on the river bank,
Scales aglint from their subterranean
Majesty but mouths round and wordless
Expressing nothing of the air they can not breathe

What a task to build a life
In bold formation
When all I was expecting was an unrolling
Of the Real McCoy

And she called it the Irresistable Seduction

TO A VAST APPLAUSE, TO A VAST APPLAUSE

Matadors of Fire! Matadors of Fire!

The music sounds irrelevant when I dance

That kind of immortality died out long ago

LAA...

ACT II

Nothing I can teach you will prepare you for that day
(pleasant enough, seductive enough) when walking here
that change is detected, an angle of a hat, a bivouacked glance,
a shadow's length, a tincture of this, of that...

                    ...until...   LAA...

YOU ARE OBLIVIOUS AND GODLESS FOR ONE WHOLE MINUTE

,   ,   ,   / /

,   ,   ,   / /

                         The dangerous opera begins

Sleep, sleep with me/

            "I WHO WAS ONCE A GOLDEN WO...
(No one can be this direct without the right music, laa)
 I was once a drummer over the sharp-breasted hills, so I should know...

                    Laa...

...I PRACTICE MY BLOOD CRIES!

            LAA_____
Matadors of Fire! Matadors of Fire!

                         The dangerous opera begins

        LAA...

    "I AM KRAKATOA"

                    sunsets will never be the same/

And so, the portions of ruined orchestration are divided equally,
As she, shamelessly naked in her mirror,
Braids her hair in a symetrical falling along the backbone
Someone is shreiking my name

But it is the silence that corrects my identity

The chorus flays: "FEAR AT THE BOTTOM OF YOUR GARDEN"

The dangerous opera begins

HARK!

those reported missing,   (dead?),

consumed by voracous clouds over uninhabited lands.... emerge....

RADIANT...

waxing the beauty of travel,

(ah, lakes glimmering on the rims of worlds unfounded in most eyes)

and the gusto of themselves / the gusto of their words

that express exact meanings /

"The wind over the reef / the red linen hills"

The chorus chanting:

THE THERAPY OF THE GODS, laa... THE THERAPY OF THE GODS

HER SIGN LANGUAGE IMPRESSED ME WITH
HOW MANY VOWELS THERE ARE IN THAT KIND
OF ALPHABET, THE "O", A CALLING THROUGH
LIPS OF WINDLESS DAYS AFLOAT, HER "U"
NOT QUITE UGLY ENOUGH TO FRIGHTEN THE
BIRDS ON THAT ROOFTOP, BUT THE VIEW FROM
HER WINDOW I COULD SEE IN MY MIND AS SHE
BENT HER FINGERS AROUND LANDSCAPES OF WORDS

So quickly their hands change my costume:

GREAT SIGHS   GREAT SIGHS
LAA...

(I have been tricked into coming this way)
LOOK! The obsequious, most loving moment!   ,   ,   ,

...with scent trailing from her...   ...beautiful...   ...body

The sky brightening from the wrong direction
Growing fat on grand anthems
    H!   ELP!

"Nimbus, O Nimbus,
Life and death go unnoticed under you"

... behind these curtains
life for that one minute was the most beautiful
        (but I can not find the outside)

I open my mouth   *LAA...*   I close it

I open my mouth   *LAA...*   I close it

I open my mouth   *LAA...*   I close it

        The street is dark

    at the far end
        I / will

      kneel down (if I may)
        and pray.

(You are waiting for me to make one mistake in my faultless singing)

The darkness teaches me to be quiet.

,   ,   ,   ,

ACT III

(A scene change)

Like

An outcry

All choirs outdo themselves
In sustaining their throats
Between degrees of waking, dreaming, dying,
And afterwards walking off... in the shoes of children

"AND WHAT HAVE YOU DONE WITH YOUR LIFE?" they sing

LAA...

(for a moment there I thought ...

                    ...**the roof would crash down on my cowry-studded headdress!**)

How we misjudge words /
their spacial occupance /
the space they accomodate /
undying /
quite heartless /
anaerobic /

And we, thinking they are unheard now (*long since left our lips*)
Believe they are dead.
It is not a coincidence that I chose *these words*

My song *will be* repeated every one hundred years (*or so*)
May 25 / 2.25 pm (*on the dot*)

I have set the words to go off at precisely this moment
Because words have all contempt for death

Not these blood-beating matadors!

(arms raised, great leaps...)

Words are heartless, silently enduring...
As we talk

The dangerous opera begins

One sublime syllable is the same as the next... if only to
                                        reach that level of listening!

DRUMS! AT LAST, DRUMS!

I try to stay awake with bravado and radiance
(Friends of mine,
Not understanding the consequences of comas
Lapse, are comforted by sleep,
Wide dreams running
Beneath their foreheads)

but not me

It is all in the headdress you wear!
(drum-shaped, sacred bird feathers spilling from the edges today)

I am alive in the streets, tackling the
Burning that passes up from within
_____ *allowing me to sing*

                    The dangerous opera begins

Work now!   Sing now!   And be graced with darkness later

Matadors of Fire! Matadors of Fire!

                Voyages, dark pastures on this isle

"I am light! I am light," she is shouting

and we will grow together
for the confines of the heart leak,
allowing the burnt earth,
fired for reasons of renewal, spring,
the first unfolding leaf,
to succour us, running into
the sea and blessing the swell and
sway of all
                                things

The dangerous opera begins

And no matter where you are
this leaking from the stitched seams
of "Our Mighty and Muscular Pumps"

(when we are young we are tidal
but growing older the sway commands
the covering of the sand. And it is quite wonderful.)

will allow me to always find you

LAA... *(7.5 / Richter Scale)*

... this singing...

this epicenter
in the center of all seas
in the smallest of alleys where
we were once and will again be wooed
where the trees were once and will again be uprooted
where the floorboards of the house were once and will again be
splayed by such a song
(as other houses have been ruined by song)

And is it worth it?

YES,

(if only to wear the much revered olivine headdress)

Yes, laa_____

alive / nothing like / dead

laa... I model myself after other great opera singers in history (who
doesn't?) / our hands seem to be the same size, (and what is it but
"hands" that is important in this opera?) / arisen in pairs / never

singularly as in defiance or shows of strength / but in pairs /
as though within each person who makes this clear gesture a
dawn has been struck, a surrender to absolutes / un-
restricted / allowing them to call out "Why, God!" / palms open / note:
never clenched in anger or mute gesticulations / but in pairs / to
forge a life apart / . . . to lift what we can not see / what we know
is there / through which we ascend. . .

       into wider spaces   *bluer*

      LAA. . .

           alive / nothing like / dead

But who will look after my headdresses?
Polish the inert metal, preen the feathered tops?
Dust the artificial fruit pouring over their haloes?

      I cry when I think of this

I have to live on.

      KRAKATOA!   **MATADORS OF FIRE!**

I open my mouth. . .   LAA. . .   I close it. . .

(Save me from going unnoticed by beautiful women.)

ACT IV

It starts, as it always does, with silence

          Very solemn   *Very intimidating*

But it's not an empty silence
It's not being asleep
It's being awake, letting doors open. . .

Nothing has happened to me. . .   that can't be altered

I've never used a script / no director can control my tiffs and tantrums

    (very childish but the only way to get

          WHAT YOU REALLY WANT!!!)

LAA. . .

TO AND FRO I GO

Wanting to tell *them* of tragedy's elopement with solemnity
Overburdening happiness hidden behind the many props
But they are either asleep or poking fun at the chorus
(*who are quite naked in a patch of dappled light, stage right*)

"OUT OF ALL THIS BEAUTY SOMETHING MUST COME"

        (*one of "them" is even making love to the*
          startling attractive usherette in the center aisle)

        A blind ritual against my riveting arias

This is how *ALONE* I am
*No one can get up after **that** right to the jaw!*

A DEVASTATION PEELING THE ROOF
FROM THE VILLAGE HUTS, A CYCLONE OF
EVENTS CULMINATING IN WORSHIP OF
THINGS UNSEEN, THE SHAKING TO THE ROOTS
OF OUR MOST HUMAN BELIEFS, TABOOS
ALLOWING ONLY THE BEAUTIFUL TO GO NAKED

        gas bills, fabrics, textures of the will, ha...

But SHE does...

Staggering into his arms (lovers menacing and jockeying for
position on her lips)

to live happily ever after

      LAA...   LAA...   LAA...

We come walking on like huge sails.

                And when death reached him /
                It was all in order /
                Passing through the Great City /
                Reciting the verses given him /
                At birth, by right of birth /
                Everything in place /
                When death reached him /

Will I too be given safe conduct through these streets?

    "There are no ifs and buts left
    The breakers over the reef
    Have given up their timely baton-beat
    Of the mortal wing. And lying here
    Amidst what decays and what remains
    Inert to change, I can find
    No gauge to the measurements
    Of my breathing..."

    But I will be remembered
    For everyone else's heroics

And, of course, my headdresses
Perched, dictatorially on my head
Rampages of swollen seas
Blizzards at the city center
Those touching moments when the girl
In the rain is rescued and smothered
In dreadful kindness, cancelling
All our invisible sins and
Backhanded compliments
Reaching a level of compression,
A small, miniature world
Dubbed "unreal" by most
But having such authenticity
In evoking emotions and true feelings
That, given the choice,
All take with both hands;
A veracity unlike anything
Known to...

And the girl crossing the road is sexually alive, laa...

(and she knows it!)

"This is no time to play dead..."

MIRACULOUSLY WALKING ON THIS LAND!

we rush in to ravage...

RADIO EUPHORIA!

LAA...   (SHUT UP!)

Matators of Fire!   Matadors of Fire!

no wonder my relationships with the
INDECENT AND BEAUTIFUL
have failed in their intensity
(true indecency is only given to those who can't appreciate its worth)

as she took off her earrings
(one by one)

and dropped them

into

his mouth

The children eat out of my hands like birds...

Each life ignites and extinguishes itself in its own window...

But it is the pageantry of each moment we love...

"over the hills and far away"

"over the hills and far away"

ACT V

"My lot in life has been to sing."

*Naturally, there have been centuries when I would have liked to
have taken a mute stance, quietly resting my huge breasts but...*

The world relies on my "but..."

"And his language, whether he knew or not, became an indigenous
poetry supplanting breastbeating as the native tongue..."

He imitated the wild unborn
(I followed in his footsteps)

HAIL, BRAVE LANGUAGES! IDENTIFY YOURSELVES!

      LAA...

          The dangerous opera begins

  ... only I understood...
      imitating the wild unborn...

*for I stand
quite unrecognizable
(like most of us)
reaching heights of the Unclasped Imagination
that my face
(blatantly normal for Act V)
never suggests
half tragedy / beyond comedy*

Overnight I have become incredibly tall...

(outstripping / in every sense /

the reputation my body has left in a land of Incessant Lovers...)

      Hailed as an ikon

O KRAKATOA!   **O KRAKATOA!**

... but infatuation dies quickly

(*the fervor of a religion based on my huge breasts is bound to be blind*

to the truth of my "real and gorgeous" being)

"NOT A CARE IN THE WORLD" (singing... laa!)

(*But I didn't read the small print*)

FOOL!

Prayer after prayer ruined (and i believe in god)
The choir, down on its knees singing_____

GREAT SIGHS!   GREAT SIGHS!

"*If you make your own bed you must die in it!*"

But our love is never like that_____ shallow,
and like most things can not be measured by
wading into the blue warm waters that fringe...
                    our deep and most lurching da...

"*Each mother knows the limits of her indurance*
passing into a land of resignation, tempered by
her childrens' goodness / that "Kiss-and-Make-Up-Country"

I TOO WAS ONCE HUNGRY, BUT YOU GET OVER IT

            ah, this living_____

            this living_____

    LAA...

(DIRECTOR'S NOTE:

            masterminding the whole scale
            of events has been beset with
            problems from before day one:
            the carpenters refusing to make
            the sea to size; the sky hammered
            together in such flimsy fashion that

as She walked beneath it, Her headdress
of abundant red coral was tilted
to an unbearable angle, clashing dreadfully
with everything natural and sacred in life;
the lyrics translated from the Italian
saying nothing, absolutely nothing,
besides the utterly inconsequential phrase:
"The Naked Seduction of the Wild Unborn"
and when I asked of this incompetance
I was told you can only translate The Word
literally, and anyway, ordinary people would be thrilled
by the mirrors of their uneventful lives suddenly shining brightly.

And then there is She,
/ those tits getting in the way of everything / everything /

everything!)

HAIL, BRAVE LANGUAGES!   IDENTIFY YOURSELVES!

my children are sheltering under my hems.

"Darling, sweetest, how many times do I have to tell you?

Don't speak with your mouth closed"

GREAT KNOWLEDGE IS LIKE THAT / TAMPERED WITH / AT THE LAST
MINUTE / LAST WORD/ LAST SENTENCE / IN THE LAST PARAGRAPH /
OF THE LAST GREAT WORK /...   Bl   uuu   rrrrr ed /

Is it the mascara running down my high cheekbones?
                (phone 03-418-1744 / ask for Venus or Mandy)
Is it the shape of my beautiful eyes?

(this portion of the show is sponsored by:
"THE UNFORGIVABLE RISK OF LIFE," quite unscheduled,
as is the sky or the sea, however precise the inevitable
lap may seem to be (quite unpredictable), that by taking
the eyes off it (life, that is) for one minute...

                we miss the whole point!
Anyway, it's all relative,
the wandering you have made
dressed in those sublime outfits

being a breed apart;
and knowing that behind you
completely missed by
facing in the wrong direction
are those experiences and landscapes
you would have preferred
if you could live life
"to the full" again

"Being a legend in my own lifetime is not difficult to live down"

(*I have left days in my life to the songwriters.*)
                              Lyrics never lie.
Setting sail on outstreched arms, singing, The Wheatfield Arias
Speaking man to man, woman to woman
Speaking man to woman, woman to man
To reproduce the entire accoustics of my "laa..."
The story of my life,
It misses the light suddenly frumbled on
In the middle of the night
To adjust a dreams storyline
Confirming fact, reassuring fiction,
Allowing a waking
To enter the sleep

SHEAVES OF SONG, HARVEST ME

Do you remember when our intelligence got in the way?
(*but today I will worship your unbelievable sexuality*)

HERE I AM

tt   tt   apping /

/   /   /   /

            /   /   /   /

                              . . . *going blind*

"QUICKEYED AND HEADLESS"
Voyages, dark pastures on this isle

244

My dances are BIG HEARTPLANTING ONES
breaking through the bushes / drunk as hell,
STAMP!　　STAMP!　　STAMPEDING
(we walked down the streets 3 girls apiece
100 men adoring her feet until…)

I WAS OBLIVIOUS AND GODLESS FOR ONE WHOLE MINUTE

The dangerous opera begins

ah, this living_____

this living_____

LAA…

Utterly beyond myself

"I WILL LIVE THROUGH THIS MASSIVE HEART ATTACK"

"Don't touch me"

"Don't touch me"

ACT VI

Of this unimaginable song. . .

> *I make my lyrics*

╌╌╌╌╌╌*╌╌╌╌╌╌*╌╌╌╌╌╌*╌╌╌╌╌╌* *(ah, barbed wire!)*

And you are asked to believe
In "Our Voyages" (*utterly beyond yourself*)
and ambitions and successes fabled to exist
But the music has become so soft that you
hear *Everything* But

"*Everything But*" (*god, I wish I'd written that song*)

ACT VII

Baby Beautiful, slowly revealed, slowly hidden.

And once I was myself
But I have changed
For better and for worse
For the song I have been forced to sing

I'm still one of the miracle kids
Who spin their hands brilliantly

I stride out under the blue eaves
My palm woven headdress
With the birds around the brim
Buffeted by the wind
Causing me to occasionally lean
Back into the past
(But my hero's welcome is long overdue
Where tomorrow is meant to come up
In a blaze of ceremony)
But of course, there is always the rerun
"The Divine Quality of the Insignificant Human Heart"
We have all seen it our countless times
But have never turned up the volume
Until chaos enters the heavens
And I stride on
(Everything becomes quite oblivious
Once you get started)

And the train will stop at stations but
The landscape is a blur, continuing to move
And death seems to make no difference
For each god we have known is too proud
To give in to stillness and silence
And the dumbfounded look on our faces
When we realize all the props covered
The same blue sky that we see now
In the rearview mirror
But we do get off
And we do walk on the green lush turf
Where I stride off
Like no natural catastrophe
Can overtake me
(I am Krakatoa, and sunsets will never be the same)

From the finest hour
To the second when
You are told how "untrue"
The irrefutable truth has been all along
You take the drama of all things seriously
Striding on to the corners of your world
In your winged shoulderblades and
Tunic of kindled blood
And the Ole! ringing from the audience
To spur you on
Striding on
Expecting at any moment
A vast flooding of ideas to imperil
Your nullness and satisfactory oblivion
So be it. So be it.

One minute will cover another
And the wake that folds over
This progression is white and new
Allowing an unheardofness to enter the vocabulary
And singularly you perceive this change
As if someone had moved the angle of light
Falling on a still life
But waiting there
Stopping the heart, listening, becoming
Quite still at the very center
The movement is detected
Following lifelines distinct and different
From the flow of the river
That has gorged the valley where
First the city builds itself up and
Is washed away, not by whim but
Will. But luckily my headdress of
Invisibility allows me to travel en force
Through the Writhing Desires, unheeded
And to myself at last, a Greatness
An everlasting likeness to my
Very own Matador of Fire

At last,
For there is never a question of an answer
When unhindered desires set forth
And we come marching on like huge sails
Laa... laa... laa...

The dangerous opera begins...

FATHER DRUM AND MOTHER NAKED LIFE

The moss breast, rainbabies, pierce the
Hands with the forest's deep red thorns
Limb-dancing in the dark vine; they comb
Their reynard earth hair with ocher-
Dipped fingernails, the great beads
Of sweet onyx around her neck
O listen to the rain in the deep resin thighs

I have cut my hair in wings, birdnape
Each palm has its own history, bark-eared and gold altared
The gong-callers crashing their hearts, the stick-dancers
The Dog Drum King shaken in leaf howls
Hands in charcoal azure, the door flung open
The stars branded on the skin

The frond girls bend: The gracious Ms. Cougar
Spiced under the earlobes chews cocoa
Massive headdresses of blood-rimmed fruit
And white-hearted epiphytes; their hands,
Arms, wrists, entangled in their hair
Rattle-life, they leap, slumberhung
And waking, every limb rooted in the dark
Fiber earth, anointment of rhythm oil

I stand in my lifetime, insect breath, white
Venom drunk: I, possessed, tainted by the
Great Wood odor. Hey, hornbill tail!
I am in love with every living movement
Taught in the drum dhetto. Smear this mud
Across the ears to dull the sound:
O but the body is lead into the dark heavens

The Shake Huts, growing in this town
I, Dappled, Almighty Heart. I, who darken
Life with the shaking of the limb tree
The red sap drinks in my throat, each

Girl a wonder flame, virgin dew, placing
Movement between languor and fervor in
The Pretty Clubs. I taste madness, a thick
Liquid welling from the Rain Drum, the world's sound

Once fire balanced on the chin, head back
Our School of Motion swayed over the Earth
Say, maracca-head, tangled Lovely One
Bring your lips into blossom range
I see the wax over the skin, needles, eyelashes
Along the eyelids, a life beaten within an
Inch of eternity. Hail, Almighty Heart, the Drum

Long live the leaf den, Voodoo Cafe, the rickety
Rhythm, it thumps like hell, body-flames jump in:
"Slush King, babe, where y' bin?"

This sprig of
Life, babe, picked
From the Limb Tree
Cloistered in dim
Hearts: we are
The Burning Armfuls

Illiterate beauty, I
Came from the forest's
Hip as the Naked Wordman
And the Rhythm Reaper
With the Dark Earth
Dancing on this
Dappled skin

Gathering me
The Wombman
Placing the Truth Root under
My tongue, I was known
As the Great Woodland
Icon, the Pale Soul

When metal was born I planted this town
I sliced down the Wonder Tree, cried
As I cut off its arms, buried its branches
Palmed mud on my temples, built the Great

251

Drum outside my heart and taught the soul
To dance "The Eternity"

The tree's grace inhabits my wrists

Through my skin the thorn talks
The fire brought from the forest
In my cheeks: Toucan Heart in
Rain hands. O teach the feet
The Little Burning Boy Dance

Father Drum and Mother Naked Life
They tore the thorn from the
Red Rhythm Tree and pressed it into
My virgin shoulders. Life ran in
The vein with the palm of the hand
On fire in the heart, life
Radiating from the Killer Drum

I, white venom drunk
Will tell the Dog Drum King's
Story. Night Peach, she head-laughs
At me, says "Me lie down in red
Feathers with girls." She true

Long Ghost, he big friend, eats
Rhythm. Shake through him
The River Tree, the earth heels
Drum ankles, he come and dance
Place needle in shoulder, see Little
Immortality, say "Good!"

Drink Drums! The bar is lined
With fire thieves; the girls place the
Most colorful leaves in the world
Over their eyes; the Father Ones are
Stripped to their tongues, the forest's
Scent ethereal behind their ears

I, Virgin Tree. You, Drum Pimp
I'm the needle-thrower, leaf wisdom
Bush lust. I blow the blossom darts
Into Night Peach's neck to keep her

Dancing, the Rhythm Tree's sap
Descending into her thighs

Ravished are we in the most
Invisible dance, oiled
Plaits simmer on the bare
Backbones. The mud painters
Are in their fury. Little
Flame Heart is mine, one
Minute on the lips, slim
Collarbones fanned out
Around their necks. O see
How we are nailed on the
Great Red Rhythm Tree

The timorous bush-guitar
Sings in the thin dark
Wrists of the Dog Drum King

Tamed fire on my shoulder
I will walk amidst these streets
Eating the forest's drug from
My hand. I will drum up the rain-
Babies, the birth of frenzy
A dance the world has yet to see

And the Dog Drum King will teach the boys to sing:

"We are the Numb Sons, the Shaken Heads."

A sonorous longing
Of their tongues
Singing the Wood
Odor Song in the
Streets, and all this
Ancient fire and
Growing, burning along
Our arms to the
Heart. Modern language
In the tree tops
Yelp from the breast

"O we are the Numb Sons, the Shaken Heads."

I, shrill, a warbler's language
Idiotic and beyond prayer and
Desire. Touch, tremble-skin
The girls mascaraed in bruised cinnabar
Gather the truth-fruits, drugged and godish
And the words I speak are the wide
Dripping fronds, the tongues of the
Great Rainwood. Ms. Cougar's kiss
Is wet with these dew-swooned words
O the city, the metalboys listen
Their ears drenched in bird pitch–
The sap's gush of song

See how the world is covered by a single leaf

Birdthroated, sweet-naped,
The tall Swoon Singers lean from
Their hearts, the honey drum
Pounds, babe. They sing:
"Feed the little white soul with fever
Grow from the body and never leave us."

"I am the Numb Son, the Shaken Head."

On my shoulders perch the Leaf Mask Gods
Sexton of the pollen, guardians of the fern's sex
King Corolla, the flaming-ready one
Sheltering my lips from luscious fire, the ears
From modern slang. See how I am a sanctuary
A home against the evil waltz, the Heartless Crowd

I am the Dog Drum King

The thorn in the Neck of Sighs
The King has come, the body is his
And the wanton sexguitar plays her
Long Limb Language, a litany of raindrugs,
Bird-drums, electric wires
See the sweet rhythm of my nakedness
Fruit-ripe god of the honey-babies

I dance. O yes, I dance

Splash the raingods on my limbs

Little Poison Thighs
A red sting of lip-light
Kissed down your neck
Mother Naked Life sighs

Sweet dart in thy hand
Kiss-men place wonder-world fingers
On lips: shh babe-rhythm
Every limb will pass through thy ecstasy

O Father Drum says so

Slim Willow is a man, Cat his kin
Kiss Man and Woman Bliss

"O we are the Numb Sons, the Shaken Heads."

Father Drum says so

A small leaf has dressed
Each earlobe. She speaks
Hornbill shrills, toucan non-
Sense Little Roosting Ones in
Arms, the Writhing Drum, lessons
In mighty motion, long whistling
Legs and the music of the Big Sway

Electrique-mud
Tongue. Drum
Heads kissing
O the world
Begins and ends in
The Big Sway

Eyelids
Bark-deepening
Open in the
Green, the bird-hall
Pierce the
Arm with loving needles

Pick up your
Scented heels in
The rustle-dance boughs
The dry leaves
Falling from her body
Leaving naked the
World for me to love

The moss breast, rainbabies, pierce the
Hands with the forest's deep red thorns

O listen to the rain in the deep resin thighs

PIERCED WITH MYSTIC SHRAPNEL

I've seen Eternity Snipers popping off Brainthrowers
In spasm taverns in Wipe Out City
Dream grenades exploding in the entombed and encoded minds
Of the Great Blab Bards of Equanimity
And Godomites on fast faith opiates spiraling
Through the aisles of Convulsion Ghetto
On Stimulation Pilgrimages among the aura-entrails
In tyranny holsters with sting stilettos

I have seen the sky pierced with mystic shrapnel
The night's Nyphetamines hung with squeal-skin drums
Figure Maters, Trigger Happies in their first Breath Throes
Sap Slobs suckling identikids, Little Squealer and Jelly Joe

I've seen Full Blasters, Aphrodisiaxes
Beautysleepers, the Varicoma Vains
Pop Slops, the Big Berserks and Slime Rhymers
Spinning mumbo-numbo tongue tales
Transplanters on vitro-crutches and Vulturians
Their 4th-eyes pulsing beneath their skins
Frenzy Sons peddling sense-kicks
And the Quag Choirs crooning the Womb Wings

I have seen the sky swirling in ol' erogenous ether
I have shone with sharpened light as I've stood beneath it
Smoked eclipse spliffs under ceilings encrusted with fiery flowers
Sacred syrups rushing through the body's full flesh tower

O I'm a wreckage on the surface
But beneath this ruined sight
Shooting through the bloodlanes
Errant atoms, haloed bright

On my forehead, alight
Plumes of phantom light
In my weakened eyes
The call of clearer sight

from
WRITING THE RIOT ACT IN THE ILLITERATE HOUR

PERFECT VISION

I am blinded by hysteric laughter
I am blinded by vicious memory
I am blinded by an ungodly darkness
I am blinded by drum-swimming air
I am blinded by cannibal jealosy
I am blinded by the mightiest drugs
I am blinded by overjoyous delinquency
I am blinded by freak language
I am blinded by a great banging
I am blinded by ravenous fire
I am blinded by the junksister's flaying song
I am blinded by sex leaps
I am blinded by the simplest goodness
I am blinded by rain killing
I am blinded by pure defiance
I am blinded by one gasp after another
I am blinded by a life of exotic furies
I am blinded by utterly abandoned ideas
I am blinded by drunk tongues
I am blinded by a choir of flaming gestures
I am blinded by moans
I am blinded by the steady derelict rhythm
I am blinded by my howling
I am blinded by opinions on everything
I am blinded by epileptic gongs
I am blinded by the juice dribbling down
I am blinded by lusthands
I am blinded by the infinite yelpdance
I am blinded by obsession
I am blinded by myself

My vision is perfect

THE OVERPOWERING URGE

The night is young
Things must be done

All your stolen jewelry around your neck
Is the tattered deeds of recklessness
The night is young
Things must be done
Put on your plundered crown
Fly around with outstretched arms
The night is young
Things must be done
Smother on your pagan make-up
The anthem of the hour is "Chaaaaarge!"
It is my last overpowering urge
To be abandoned under a life-sized sky
Carried up all shoulder high
Singing "I will never die"

The night is young
Things must be done

All your skin-shaped beauty will not redeem
The rifled pleasures split at the seams
The night is young
Things must be done
Comb up the crazy tumults
Sit all soaked in sexual drums
The night is young
Things must be done
And I will pour into your open ear
The anthem of the hour is "Chaaaaarge!"
It is my last overpowering urge
To be abandoned under a life-sized sky
Carried up all shoulder high
Singing "I will never die"

THE PIECES

These are the pieces

Choose ones that won't decay
Choose ones that have hectic sexuality sometimes
That are not kissable right now
That are not lovable right now but will endure
I can wait, I have always waited for you

One house is enough to house them

Choose ones that are resilient
Choose ones most indecent in their movements
That are pleasant on reflection
That are bright with saving graces
I will wait, I will always wait for you

One house is enough to house them

FALCON MAN'S BIG LEAP

Falcon Man's big leap
Leaves the earth behind

Grows his wings upon his shoulderblades
Stains his skin with indigo
Drinks the white juice of the nightshade
Knows the passage of the sun
See we dance like birds around him so
O we squawk and now we sing
Hear the words of incantation come
As his heels provide the spring

Falcon Man's big leap
Leaves the earth behind

And so he sees the glory
Of the festooned fields below him
The houses of our lives there
The smallness of our hearts
See him laugh and tremble
Spread his wings untethered
Our eyes are pierced with visions
We place our hands together

Flying out now
He shakes
Colored in feathers
Leaping
Over the treetops
We here
Fear of his shadow
Moving
Sweeps down
Over this country
Our eyes

Drugged in wonder
We who
All of his stories
Singing

O we pass around the naked songs
Tell our children of his name
The story moves within our families
How he left the body in a flock of flame

How he alights upon our foreheads
How he dives into our eyes
To teach our tongues tradition
Of inner skies to fly

DANCE THE GREAT DELIRIUM

The Sweet Toxin Things, corrupted on eruption snuff, sing:

The music is a lash-sh-sh / whip it / crack it /
Spit the rhythm down / take it home / trash it /
Tenderness waits with her dress all ripped
"Come to Bedlam" dripping from her lips

The first 4 bars of life are fired up / shot down /
You with y' big mouth / yelp out / sex-howls /
All you want to do is burn down the day
"Come to Bedlam" is all baby can say

The Cosmic Epileptic Acrobats are torturing sleaze trumpettes with Jelly Jive

The denunciation drugs are good, cascading in the flesh
The full-bodied whines are loud, the jolt scents fresh
Put the Baffle Root beneath your tongue
And leap through the Squirm as the cages are sprung

Get out y' drums… drums… drums… they're burning down Bedlam

With y' shiny skull calipers, y' optick braces
Y' can dance The Great Delirium
In y' flaming spurs through the Slitherland hum
U too can do The Blackout, son

Sloppy on y' feet / wired up / wrecked out /
Haunting down the streets / heart's all ripped out /
All the fires are burning beneath the sheets
"Come to Bedlam" is all baby can speak

And the Sweet Toxin Things, swaddled in their neuro-slings, sing:

Get out y' drums, get out y' drums
And dance The Great Delirium
Get out y' drums, get out y' drums
And dance The Great Delirium

SACRED FEVERS

Here is the heat of the sacred fever
Wrapped around the head
In and out of the Rhythm Almighty I go
Affected...
Infected...
Let me be a dance unto myself

Sacred fevers are flowing like rivers
Sacred fevers wash over me
Sacred fevers are unleashed in the body
Sacred fevers love everybody

Here in the oblivious second, I shake
Remove these spiritual bandages
Once I subside I start again, without end
Weave...
Careen...
Let me be a dance unto myself

Through the fields we reap havoc
I am a dance unto myself—touch me
We can drink, but we will thirst
I am a dance unto myself—touch me
Through the doors we will burst
I am a dance unto myself—touch me
I was given these fevers, I writhe, this is life
I am a dance unto myself—touch me

Sacred fevers are flowing like rivers
Sacred fevers wash over me
Sacred fevers are unleashed in the body
Sacred fevers love everybody

BRINGING HOME
THE SINGING FIRE

The willow sways
Raising up its arms above the earth
To show
That the virgin life that grows
Is the fire that we all hold
And we go now, planting dances to life

O how the dancers
They seem to wrap
Their arms around you

The magnolia's heart
Wonderously white upon the branch
It blooms .
"O my beauty it will change
Yet the world will still remain."
And we go now, planting dances to life

O how the dancers
They seem to wrap
Their arms around…

You, who have brought the singing fire
Here placed it back into our hearts
Know that to love and hear
The songs that feed us
Planted by the river .
Are the ones that never leave us

O as we walk upon the fields
O as we stand beneath the trees
See we are young
And we are old with memories

Arms around each other
The hearts inside all lovers
Bringing home the singing fire

I have opened hearts
Where there has been honey in the comb
And known
That the sweetness in my hands
Is dripping down into this land
And we go now, planting dances to life

How long I've waited
I see you come to me now
Bringing home here
Laid in your hands
The singing fire

THE KNIFETHROWER, THE MAGNIFICENT

Do not tremble, do not move
Stand quite still—now I will blindfold you

I am the Knifethrower, the Magnificent

This knife is for the drowning night
This knife is for the clustered stars
This knife is for every raw emotion
That leaves a wound but not a scar

This knife is for your beautiful eyes
This knife is for your parted mouth
This knife is for the desires that burn
Than can not be described in words

This will not hurt, you may never feel it at all
Ah, but I am the knifethrower
So when I pierce your heart
Fall wilted into my arms

On every finger are the rings
Of envy, agony, and sin
The hand that rises with the blade
Never wavers in its aim

Don't be afraid, I'll spin you around
Trust me, I have never missed

This last knife is my life

SEXIETY

Slopped on the bed in flaming sleep
The two-bit cherub and the muscular meet
Hear the sigh against the ear
The cracking sound of each heart beat
This thirst: obsession, this hunger: possession
The pains of love will never lessen

I'm the Most Beautiful Woman in the World
I cry for what can not be preserved
This pairing up, this stripping down
The unleashing of the Emotional Hounds
You be the hunter, I'll be the prey
Or should we try it the other way?

These are the deeds, these are the creeds of s-s-s-sexiety

Soft the skin, moist the lips
Take these arms, come to grips
I'll confess, you deceive
Sensual games of make-believe

The Pleasure Manual is ripped and torn
I've been the rose and you the thorn
In the infinite arenas of experiment
The mystery's muted, the veil is rent
A moment the hunter, the next the prey
Or darling, should we try it the other way?

These are the seeds, these are the needs of s-s-s-se-se-sexiety

271

WATER FOR A BARREN HEART

Crumble
Into my arms
And find rest
I pour in
Through your heart
That is loveless

I am water
That is washing away
The new
It will unfold,
The old, decays

In the Days of Frenzy, Days of Fury
Oh, what cures you—cures me

Out in the fields the lovers sow
Till the barren heart is made to grow

I see
Your little world
Is cracked and dry
You and your walking
Too near the fire

I am water
That is washing away
The new
It will unfold
The old, decays

I will plant you by the water
In the Season of the Soul
I will plant you by the water
I have come to make you whole

In the Days of Frenzy, Days of Fury
Oh, what cures you—cures me

Out in the fields the lovers sow
Till the barren heart is made to grow

IKONIC

Burn the Gong Cinema and the Trance Halls

LEAPING THROUGH FIERY HOOPS

I'm dressed in my sublime longing
See my coat of Great Desire
Passion-tipped arrows strapped to my back
And my blazing eyes

I stride into the ring
Majestic as a horse
I bring down the house
To thunderous applause

I am the immaculate animan
Who eats out of your hand
With a snap of your fingertips
I will perform fantastic tricks

Leaping through fiery hoops

Leaping through fiery hoops for you
There is nothing I will not do

I'm dangerous when I'm alone
Rearing up in tossing plumes
But you calm my savage instincts
Without you, I am extinct

I am the immaculate animan
Who eats out of your hand

Leaping through fiery hoops for you
There is nothing I will not do

FOREVER BURSTING INTO FLAME

All these everlasting looks
They disappear from year to year
Every beauty has its day
But distant thunder's always near

All these everlasting looks
All this beating on the drum
One look now, one look away
The moments of the night are young

All these... but after all
It's not how many hearts you kill
Eternity is all uphill
Desire may walk upon these shores
But washed away is soon ignored

Only you, only you remain the same
Forever bursting into flame

Only you remain unchanged
A constant in the passing days

Only you remain the same
Forever bursting into flame

THE LIGHT YEARS

It don't bite, this... light
It goes right through y', makes y' high
Let it in through y' eyes
It'll blow y' mind

Don't fight it, enjoy it
Just lie back, you'll feel inert. Does it work?
Y' gonna slide away
Slam out y' day
Ain't it kinda cute... reds, yellas, blues

Don't fake it, you'll love it
It's bliss, like some... perfect kiss
It's gonna wipe the day clean
Make y' 'ave great dreams
O this light, it's kinda white
Don't fight it, enjoy it

I'm travellin' over oceans
I'm tangled in new emotions
I've bin places y' won't believe
I'm 'avin' the strangest dreams

I'm seein' things, I'm feelin' things
I'm blackin' out, where's m' mouth?
I feel nothin', I'm out of it
Where did y' get this light?
It's so pure, so white

Don't be scared, I'll take care o' y'
Where am I? You're fine
Don't fight it. Enjoy it

I'm driftin' away
Nothin' will be the same

I'm a million miles away...
I'm King Blade, the Idiot Heart
I'm Blue Rinse, the Galactic Tart
I'm Whip Lash, the Wonder Head
I'm Rip Blam, the Miracle Kid
I'm Slang Burns, the Mighty Mouth
I'm Little Smash, the Giant Dreamer
I'm Bitch Him, the Colossal Dent
I'm Sex Reader, the Ulti-mate
I'm Trash Lip, the Lingo-Go
I'm Drum Babe, the Great Glow
I'm Jane Rough, the Oblivious
I'm Swoon Rhythm, the Fire Hunter
I'm Cry Iron, the Scar Song
I'm Sugarcane, the Dance Trap
I'm Bright Thigh, the Rapture
I'm Myth Yelp, the Erotic Angel
I'm Slap Happy, the Thud Club
I'm Beat Kiss, the Crashing Life
I'm Bullet Man, the Mouthful
I'm Crazy Ray, the Naked Truth
I'm Art Howl, the Genuine Thing
I'm Nectar Girl, the Unnatural
I'm Slip Hip, the Smoking Language
I'm Dog Fear, the Endless Spirit
I'm Body Sister, the Dreaming Women
I'm Pop Self, the Stupid Season
I'm Ping-Pong, the Emblazoned Idea
I'm Sing Wife, the Wafer Thin

Baby, don't you know me?
Baby, don't you see?
Baby, just believe in what I can be

I'm travellin' over oceans
I'm tangled in new emotions
I've bin places y' won't believe
I'm 'avin' the strangest dreams

I'm driftin' away
Nothin' will be the same
I'm a million miles away...

FROM THE RUINS
OF YOUR BEAUTIFUL BODY,
THE LIGHT OF DAY

In the ruins of your beautiful body, I'll find you
And all your sacred abuse
Is the tightning of a noose
You wear like a rosary to keep your emotions at bay

And in the rubble I build a fire, to warm you
And there are feelings alive
In the depravity of your eyes
That open, as do arms, reaching to grab at straws

I am here to crack the ice in the coldest hour
I am here to bring back life to a wilted flower

From the ruins of your beautiful body, I am the light of day

Is this what remains?
Is this what we must build again?
Is this what stands?
Is this what needs a helping hand?

In the ruins of your beautiful body, I call you
I'm the voice you love best
I'm the heart in your own chest
For where there's a way to die, there is a will to live

From the ruins of your beautiful body, I am the light of day

HAVING TO FIND A NOBLE LANGUAGE

The waiters serve helleborus, dolphin-arc, and rhythm drugs:

"I will live forever."

THE BIG BLISS

I have nothing more to say _____ that's it!

I am graced with these silent lips
I will put my tongue into your cheek
I will act all spineless and sort of weak
And I will live with what I'll miss
For honey-babe, ignorance is bliss

There's a shutter on the window
A seal upon the door
And I will shut myself inside my shell
O Sugar, all is well that ends well...

I have nothing more to say _____ that's it!
There are no words for this
For this is, this is, this is... the Big Bliss

Remember when you didn't give a heck
Blessed in all your anointed recklessness?
Remember the dying swan in your arms
All those screaming sirens and alarms?

But you must forget all this
I will make it so white and pure
Now isn't that better? Aren't you cured?
O hush baby, hush. What's all the fuss?
You silly thing _____ you silly thing
Forget all this...
Without a word, with a kiss
Forget all this...
For this is, this is, this is... the Big Bliss

That's it!

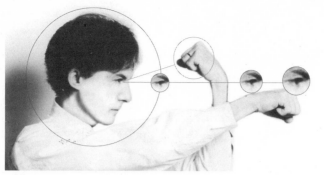

BOY ABYSS

Lyricist Chris Mosdell has written for Eric Clapton, Boy George, Ryuichi Sakamoto and Yellow Magic Orchestra. He has co-written with Michael Jackson; collaborated on film scores, operatic works and theatrical productions; and been commissioned to write the election theme song for the Social Democratic Party of Japan. In addition to winning the Gold Prize at the Tokyo Music Festival for his lyrics, Mosdell has been awarded the Yuki Hayashi-Newkirk Poetry Prize and, most recently, the Grand Prize for Poetry at the Boulder, Colorado, Festival of Literature. The innovator of "Visic," a development of visual music, his groundbreaking work culminated in the interactive audio-visual album *Equasian*. In collaboration with the poet Shuntaro Tanikawa, he also wrote *The Oracles of Distraction*, a set of ideographic cards adjoined to musical functions, and composed the musical soundtrack for the gallery installations of Graham Hancock's best-selling book, *Fingerprints of the Gods*.